# NINE WHO CHOSE AMERICA

*Nine*

Compiled by the Editors of LIFE International

# WHO CHOSE *America*

Illustrated with photographs

E. P. DUTTON & COMPANY, INC., NEW YORK

Not like the brazen giant of Greek fame,
With conquering limbs astride from land to land;
Here at our sea-washed, sunset gates shall stand
A mighty woman with a torch, whose flame
Is the imprisoned lightning, and her name
Mother of Exiles.

.    .    .    .    .

"Send these, the homeless, tempest-tossed to me,
I lift my lamp beside the golden door!"

Emma Lazarus
From *The New Colossus*, 1883

# Contents

# Introduction

AMONG the man-made shrines and hallowed places of the world's nations the one best known and most loved by Americans is the Statue of Liberty. Given by the people of France to those of America in 1884, "Miss Liberty" holds aloft a lighted torch three hundred feet above the harbor in New York City, in symbolic welcome to America. The American, whether he is making a routine daily trip across the harbor or returning home by plane or ship from the Old World, can scarcely look upon Frédéric Auguste Bartholdi's great figure, weathered and streaked by Atlantic winds, without recalling the lines by Emma Lazarus that are inscribed on the statue's base:

> *Give me your tired, your poor,*
> *Your huddled masses yearning to breathe free,*

*The wretched refuse of your teeming shore.*
*Send these, the homeless, tempest-tossed, to me,*
*I lift my lamp beside the golden door!*

Here as in no other American place is evoked the spirit of a nation drawn, in a short span of years, from all nations—and that draws in turn from its diverse origins the underlying spirit of its unity. That spirit was expressed in 1782 by a French-born farmer named Michel Guillaume Jean de Crèvecoeur as well as it can be expressed today: *"He* is an American who, leaving behind him all his ancient prejudices and manners, receives new ones from the new mode of life he has embraced, the new government he obeys, and the new rank he holds. He becomes an American by being received in the broad lap of our great *Alma Mater.* Here individuals of all nations are melted into a new race of men, whose labors and posterity will one day cause great changes in the world."

The day of those "great changes" has arrived. It has arrived both because of the fact that America became a "melting pot" and because of the nature of the peoples who made it so.

They came from every part of the world, bringing their national characteristics and infusing them into one new national character which was unlike any in the world yet which contained parts of all the world. More important was the one element that seemed to dominate the old character and the new. It was that spirit which led them to break off their roots and make the long, uncomfortable, often perilous journey to an unknown land. All visualized the New World as a glittering goal. Yet all realized that the way to the goal was hard.

They realized the way was hard, but they took it. And that is what, more than any other single element, has made the greatest contribution to America's growth. It was their courage and eagerness to accept the challenge that led them to America, their courage and eagerness to accept all challenge that made America great.

In this book are the life stories of some of the most famous American immigrants. Their stories are collected from a series of articles written for LIFE International, the English language edi-

tion of LIFE which circulates overseas. These nine people were selected for the series because their particular stories most clearly
illustrated what America has offered the immigrant and what the
immigrant has contributed to America. Many famous foreign-born
Americans have been omitted because their rise to eminence was
achieved before coming to the United States. The series was concerned with those who made their success—and thus their unique contribution—in this country. And the ones included here are only
the most conspicuous examples, representing the many millions like
them who have settled in America. Like those millions, those
described here did indeed find America a "golden door." But like
other millions, their gain was America's too.

Much of America's pioneering in the air can be credited to
Russian-born Igor Sikorsky. Law in the United States is durable
and yet warmly human, partly because of such Supreme Court
Justices as Austrian-born Felix Frankfurter. A maker of some of
those laws has recently been a United States Congressman, born in
India, named Dalip Saund. America, and the world, is richer for
the operas of Italian-born Gian Carlo Menotti, the universally popular songs of Russian-born Irving Berlin. American women are a joy to
behold largely because beauty is a serious concern of such Americans
as Polish-born Helena Rubinstein. Working Americans can be
thankful for the wise labor leadership of Polish-born David Dubinsky. The rest of the world has come to share America's pleasure in
the entertainment genius of Greek-born moviemaker Spyros Skouras.
And millions of peoples everywhere are alive today because of the
brilliant discoveries of Russian-born microbiologist Selman Waksman.

Virtually all of these new Americans made their great contributions despite considerable obstacles. Their America was not the land
of ease, as many had heard. But, as all had heard, it was indeed the
land of opportunity. Sikorsky writes: "I have been hungry in America. I have known what it is to seek for work and not find it in America. But there was never a day during the hardest times that I lost hope
in my planes or that I did not say aloud, 'Thank God I am here, a

free man, breathing free air. No man can order what I do. If I fail I can try again!' " It was this combination, the stimulation of adversity and the spur of opportunity, which led Sikorsky, and the others like him, on to great achievements. The nine people described in this book, and the other millions not so well known, came to America because they were the kind to rise to such opportunity, to rise above such adversity. They have contributed to America's industry, to her literature, to her arts, to her sense of humor, to her broader understanding of the world abroad, to every aspect of American life.

No country in history has experienced such tides of immigration. In one period, for example, between 1840 and 1900, more than eighteen million people passed the portals of the "golden door." Today there is a great deal of controversy in America over the quotas and restrictions of United States immigration laws; but the controversy tends to obscure the fact that immigrants continue to enter the country in impressive numbers: 260,000 last year, and more than 2,500,000 since 1945. In fact, as Archibald MacLeish points out in his article on Frankfurter, *all* Americans are immigrants, in a sense. America was founded by men and women with spirit and determination and broad horizons, who came to the New World to make a better home than they could in the Old. So have new Americans, with the same spirit, determination and broad horizons, come here ever since. And they have not simply made America a better place. They have made America.

The Editors of
LIFE International

# NINE WHO CHOSE AMERICA

*Igor Sikorsky*

# Igor Sikorsky

*I have been hungry in America. I have known what it is to seek for work and not find it in America. But there was never a day during the hardest times that I lost hope in my planes or that I did not say aloud, "Thank God I am here, a free man, breathing free air. No man can order what I do. If I fail I can try again!"*

*by* L E S T E R   B E R N S T E I N

# To the New World for New Wings

THE classic United States immigrant comes to America's shores out of a squalid past. He is a kind of battered cipher yearning for freedom and opportunity to make something of himself for the first time.

Igor Ivanovich Sikorsky carried only a single suitcase and $600 when he sailed past the Statue of Liberty in 1919, and it was his yearning to be free that made him flee the Communist Revolution in his native Russia. But behind Sikorsky, then only twenty-nine, lay a well-born past, a self-earned fortune and pioneering achievement that already assured him a place in aviation history. Despite this illustrious background, he was jobless and short of funds. Unknown in a strange land, he faced obstacles even greater than those he scaled in his first career. Sikorsky started over again—and built a career more brilliant than the first.

*After his arrival in the United States in 1919, Sikorsky walks a New York street.*

As designer and builder of ever larger aircraft in the United States, Sikorsky triumphed during the 1930s with the great Flying Clippers that blazed the trail of transoceanic air travel. Then after going at least as far as any of his contemporaries in pursuit of man's age-old dream of flying like the birds, he performed a more revolutionary aeronautical feat. To him goes the major credit for enabling man to fly as few birds ever could—backward as well as forward, straight up or down, sideways in any direction, inching a safe path through fog or snow, even hanging stock-still in mid-air or poised a foot above the ground. Sikorsky, a completely modest man, speaks without boastfulness when he calls his helicopter "the most universal vehicle ever created by man, from the pack mule to the jet plane."

For all of Sikorsky's genius for surpassing himself, the helicopter seems to be his crowning achievement. In the spring of 1957, on his sixty-eighth birthday, he retired from the United Aircraft Corporation's Sikorsky Division, where he had held the unassuming title of engineering manager since 1929, when he forsook the business side of airplane manufacturing to concentrate on his creative role and to indulge a personality that he considered unsuited to the usual cut-and-thrust of executive life.

Courteous to a fault, Sikorsky has never been known by his associates to raise his voice, pound a table, or lose his temper. His gentle, professorial air suggests nothing of the steely tenacity that has propelled his lifelong effort to conquer the air. And Sikorsky's retirement, which conformed to the company policy on age, might have been just as deceptive. He continued "indefinitely" with the company as a consultant. Bald-domed with a scraggly gray mane, a tufty mustache, and wise gray-green eyes, he remained vigorously active. His erect, portly figure popped up on helicopter business in Los Angeles, Brussels, and Caracas.

Though it is the latest of his contributions to flight, the helicopter is the first aircraft that Sikorsky ever tried to build—and, indeed, the very notion of it was his first inkling that man might fly at all. One of his earliest recollections of his boyhood in Kiev, where he was born May 25, 1889, the youngest of five children, was his mother's story of Leonardo da Vinci's attempts to design a spiral airscrew that would fly straight up. That was even before his eleventh year, when he was inducted into the mysteries of electricity, astronomy, and physics by his father, a brilliant psychology professor and physician. At twelve, young Igor managed to put together a model helicopter that flew under the power of a rubber band. He was fourteen when Wilbur and Orville Wright left the ground for the first time in December 1903. "It was less than twenty-four hours after I heard of it," he recalls, "that I made the decision to go into aviation."

Young Igor postponed acting on the decision only long enough to get some schooling, though not long enough to get a degree. After three years at the Naval College in St. Petersburg and while still a student at the Kiev Institute of Technology, he determined to build a helicopter. He was nineteen. With a loan from his older sister, Olga, he set off for Paris, then the mecca of European aviation, to buy an engine and get some pointers. In the Juvisy airfield outside Paris, he lost himself in aviation's brave new world of struts, wires, and wood. The crates sputtered and lurched across the pasture, belching the smoke of burning castor oil. But few rose in the air. Everyone advised him against trying a helicopter. But Sikorsky bought himself an engine and prepared to return home to start work.

For the next two and a half years, Sikorsky risked his neck to make his aircraft fly. His family went heavily into debt and even staked its home as collateral so he could build new ones when he climbed out of the wreckage. Flying the planes was just as much a pioneering venture as designing them, and Sikorsky learned both skills by a kind of spontaneous do-it-yourself method. Long after there were test pilots to perform the trials, he clung to the rule, still unbroken, of piloting every plane he ever put together.

But it took many trips back to the drawing board before he built a plane that would get into the air. His first helicopter roared and tugged and managed by Sikorsky's measurements to exert a lifting force of 357 pounds. Unfortunately, that was a hundred pounds less than its own weight. The machine, as he later wrote, "was a failure to the extent that it did not fly." He built a second, more powerful helicopter, ordering the propeller from the carpenter who repaired his family's broken furniture. It also refused to fly. He decided to give up helicopters "temporarily." It was thirty years before he finally was able to make one fly.

Sikorsky's next venture, his first fixed-wing plane, the S-1, never got off the ground. His second, the S-2, stayed in the air for hops so short that they were reckoned in seconds; its flying time came to a total of eight minutes when he tried his first turn and crashed in a ravine. Sikorsky nursed his cuts and bruises and toiled over plans for the S-3. When that plane cracked up after logging seven minutes, he went off to brood over whether to give the whole thing up. Then he stubbornly began building two planes at once. One of them, the S-5, gave him what he regards as his first real flight: it lasted four minutes, reached an altitude of 300 feet, and made a good landing. It was the S-5 which, with a mosquito, gave him the

*Biplane built in 1911 won Sikorsky a prize and a job.*

idea for a multiengined plane. The plane's motor suddenly sputtered to a halt at an altitude of 150 feet and Sikorsky managed to scramble out of a forced landing. He pulled the engine apart to discover what had gone wrong. He found that a mosquito had been drawn into the tiny jet of the carburetor, blocking the gasoline supply and proving almost too dramatically that safety demanded more than one engine. It was not until his sixth plane won the highest award at a Moscow aircraft exhibition in 1912 that Sikorsky's efforts began to produce any income. By then, his family's loans came to $25,000, a sum he soon managed to repay in full.

The prize-winning plane also won twenty-three-year-old Sikorsky the post of designer and chief engineer of a new aircraft division of the Russian Baltic Railroad Car Works. There he built the first multiengined plane, "The Grand," a four-engined craft with a wing-spread of ninety-two feet and such features as a washroom and a balcony where passengers could take a turn in the open air. It was

*Larger four-engine plane, 1914, led to wartime bombers.*

inspected by Czar Nicholas II, who chatted with Sikorsky about the plane and later sent him a diamond-studded gold watch and chain. Symbolically, in Sikorsky's home today, an oil painting of The Grand is flanked by a large framed copy of the Declaration of Independence. His next plane, an even larger version of The Grand, proved the most successful bomber of World War I. He built seventy-five of them; only one went down in combat. Then production—and the whole world of Sikorsky's upbringing, striving, and success—was brought to a dead halt by the Revolution.

Sikorsky was thrown into idleness and growing despondency over the future. Several of his closest friends were executed by the Communists. With others he spent many brooding hours discussing his prospects. He felt that there could be no free creative work in Russia for a long time and particularly that there was no place for his own skill and experience.

Without waiting to notify his friends he took the train from Petrograd to Murmansk and boarded a steamer for England. Behind him lay all he had earned in nine years of work—$500,000 in real estate and government bonds. Though his mother had died by then and he had lost a brother in the war, he left behind all of his other relatives, including a sister; many members of his family were later to follow him to the United States. "I felt the immensity of the tragedy," says Sikorsky, "and realized that my individual loss was insignificant compared to it." After a brief stay in London, he went to Paris, where he spent a year designing bombers for the French, but the Armistice was signed before any of these machines could be finished. Then, says Sikorsky, "partly because of what I had heard of it and partly by intuition, I decided to go to the United States and try to start life again." He sailed on the French ship *Lorraine* and landed in Manhattan on a clear, chilly March day in 1919.

"The United States," Sikorsky has written in his autobiography, "seemed to me the only place which offered a real opportunity in what was then a rather precarious profession. I had been inspired by the work of Edison and Ford, the realization that a man in this country, with ideas of value—and I hoped that mine were—might have a chance to succeed. . . . When I first saw New York, with the skyscrapers, subways, busy streets, and bright lights . . . I felt that it was important. In one week I was at home in its dynamic atmosphere and feverish activity. I liked it in spite of the fact that, in elegance and dignity, London and old Petrograd were, to my mind, far superior. New York was more alive."

But Sikorsky, whose English was even more limited than his funds or his contacts, found that United States aviation did not rush to make him welcome. Indeed, the industry slumbered in a twilight between dismantling its wartime operations and beginning its peacetime expansion. After two short-lived designing jobs, the young immigrant's $600 savings began melting away while he hunted for work. He moved from a comfortable hotel to a cheap two-room apartment, then to a single furnished room in lower Manhattan at $6 a week. For the first time in his life, he began to experience hunger. Lunch and dinner usually consisted of a cup of coffee and a plate of Boston baked beans, a meal then available in a modest New York restaurant for twenty cents. "Bread and butter were free," recalls Sikorsky, "and I was still able to leave five cents for the girl and feel like a gentleman."

What enabled Sikorsky to keep going and to achieve his United States success was not only the traditional formula—his own talent and initiative, and the climate of free opportunity—but the help of other immigrants, many of whom rose with him. Unable to find an aviation job, he brushed up on his mathematics and began teaching it at the Russian Collegiate Institute to Russian immigrants, most from New York's lower East Side. Soon, through contacts he made there, he was getting invitations to lecture on aviation and astronomy before immigrant groups. The lectures paid from $3 to $10 and often entailed lugging a heavy slide projector a mile or two from outlying subway stations. But the fees kept him in baked beans. More than that, the talks enabled Sikorsky, who proved an able lecturer, to infect his audiences with his own desire to build airplanes. It was largely among these groups that he found the workmen and small investors who pooled their meager savings and joined him in launching the Sikorsky Aero Engineering Corporation, just four years after his arrival in the United States. It was also among the fellow immigrants on his lecture circuit that he met a night-school teacher named Elizabeth Semion, who had been born of Russian parents in the Far East and had arrived in the United States a year after Sikorsky. They were married in 1924.

During the four years spent working toward his return to aviation, Sikorsky devoted his spare time to designing new planes. Since his one-room flat was cold and lighted only by a single small window, his drawing board often consisted of a table in the well-heated New York Public Library, where he also reread the novels of Dostoevski.

Most of his sketching in the library pointed toward the first plane that he actually built in the United States. But beyond this, he drew much bigger, four-engined planes with room for forty or fifty passengers. "During those trying years," he reminisces, "I was building in my imagination, and sometimes working out on paper, the airplanes which I have built and which have flown the oceans." Sikorsky, who is something of a mystic and a deeply religious member of the Russian Orthodox Church, has speculated at length on where his inventive ideas come from and why they sometimes cannot be explained rationally until years afterward. For example, he used the long, narrow wing shape years before he was aware of the aerodynamic basis for such a design. He has concluded that he, like other successful inventors, has been able to glimpse the future through a "mysterious faculty" of intuition.

How Sikorsky managed to get his first United States design built is perhaps even more remarkable than the mystery of its intuitive conception. He began construction with less than $1,000. The site was a onetime chicken coop near Long Island's Roosevelt Field on a farm owned by one of the workmen who was also a charter stockholder. Sikorsky's men bought a secondhand drill press for $1.80 and scavenged in the local junk yard to get angle irons from discarded bedsprings and a fifty-cent automobile bumper that they made into big shears for cutting sheet metal. They bought other parts from army surplus supplies and in five-and-ten-cent stores. When some of the makeshift odds and ends did not fit, Sikorsky redrew the blueprints. Most of the workmen were Russian immigrants; without money for a hangar, they toiled on the plane outdoors in weather so wintry that their hands stuck to the cold metal. When they managed at last to rent a hangar at Roosevelt Field, it was thanks to another, more affluent immigrant. A $5,000 contribution came from Sikorsky's good friend, Serge Rachmaninoff, the composer and pianist, who thereupon became vice president of the company.

By the time the plane was ready to fly, nobody had been paid for twenty weeks and the company could not afford a barrel of gasoline for the fuel tanks. "Somehow," says Sikorsky, "we got a few cans of it from the neighboring filling station." The plane was wheeled out rather gingerly; Sikorsky fretted over its used tires as well as the two secondhand wartime engines that were neither powerful nor reliable enough for the craft. "I wanted to take only three men," he recalls, "but seven or eight crowded into the airplane. It was a mistake. I knew it at the time, but did not have the heart to put them out after all their efforts." Within seconds from the take-off, the plane went into a forced landing, struck a ravine, and suffered heavy damage, though nobody was badly hurt. "This is the end," said one of Sikorsky's close associates.

Sikorsky determined to repair the plane, and his loyal staff went on working without pay. By a lucky stroke, about that time newspaper reporters began flocking to that part of the field to cover exhibitions by a French war ace; they used the telephone at the Sikorsky hangar frequently and paid for their calls. Sikorsky's workmen used the change to buy milk and bread as a basic diet. But they also needed new engines. Sikorsky called a special meeting of the fifty stockholders (mostly Russians) who were still speaking to him. When they had crowded into his small office, he made an unaccustomed dramatic gesture. He turned the key in the door with a loud click and announced: "That door will not be unlocked until $2,500 is subscribed." The money was raised, and a new pair of overhauled engines purchased.

In September 1924, sternly permitting only three others aboard, Sikorsky took the S-29-A up for a successful flight. In all, the plane was to fly more than 500,000 miles. It could carry fourteen passengers and cruise at 100 mph. It was one of the first twin-engined aircraft built in the United States capable of flying on one engine. And it put Igor Sikorsky back into aviation.

The success of the S-29-A brought Sikorsky new financing in hundreds of thousands of dollars, but the company struggled along modestly for several years, finding few customers for planes and suffering some jarring setbacks. Sikorsky's first effort at an amphibian ended in a crash, and a trimotor plane that he built for a transatlantic flight went up in flames in a take-off accident. In 1927 he managed to build a serviceable twin-engined amphibian, and in 1928—when aviation began booming in the aftermath of Charles Lindbergh's Atlantic crossing—he turned out a still better one, the S-38, a ten-seater. The U.S. Navy ordered two after a test pilot found the S-38's performance better than any other plane of its size and power. Pan American Airways bought others to start its routes in South America, and private orders followed. In all, Sikorsky sold more than a hundred of the planes and attracted Wall Street financing to reorganize the company into a $5,000,000 firm. Soon afterward the company was sold to United Aircraft, and its activity expanded even more dramatically as Sikorsky began building his huge flying boats. The first was the four-engined, seventeen-ton S-40, built for Pan American and dubbed the American Clipper. Next, in 1934, came the twenty-ton Clipper, the S-42, which pioneered the air routes across both the Pacific and the Atlantic and opened a new era in travel.

*In mid 1930s Sikorsky posed with Clipper that pioneered ocean air routes.*

Through the years when he was becoming famous for his amphibians and Flying Clippers, the helicopter whirred insistently at the back of Sikorsky's mind. It developed slowly but persistently. "I am a grain of sand in an oyster," Sikorsky once told friends, "and around this grain of sand a pearl, known as the helicopter, has been developed." In 1929, he set down drawings in the pages of his neat ledgers bearing a close family resemblance to his present "whirlybirds." In 1931, he patented his helicopter design. In 1937, the year that Germany's Heinrich Focke built a helicopter that stayed in the air for an hour and twenty minutes, Sikorsky rose at a meeting of United executives and announced that the time had come to put his design to the test.

Out of respect for Sikorsky, the United executives reluctantly consented to let him try. They knew that the helicopter had proved a tantalizing will-o'-the-wisp through centuries of trial and error. Weird contraptions had been put together, only to founder on aerodynamic quirks. Because a whirling rotor blade has more lift as it sweeps forward into the wind than on its backward journey, the craft tended to roll over sideways. With the turning of the rotor, torque tended to whirl the body of the helicopter in the other direction. Also, a spinning rotor was much the same as a gyroscope—which resists any movement from its original position. Still another formidable problem was an effective steering mechanism for a machine intended to fly in all directions.

Sikorsky set to work with his old intensity—and as frugally as if the company were a down-at-heel Russian emigrant group instead of an important part of a multimillion-dollar corporation. His first model was "the sketch of an aircraft," a squat framework of welded pipes, containing a motor and topped by a rotor. There was only one way to find the flaws in it. Sikorsky had the craft tethered to the ground with stout ropes, then climbed into the seat in his dark business suit and upturned fedora and tried to learn how to make it fly. On the first trial in which the machine left the ground, it lurched sideways "like a frightened horse." In all, the little craft went through nineteen major alterations before Sikorsky perfected it and, in 1941, set a flight endurance record of one hour and forty-two minutes. He received U.S. helicopter pilot's license No. 1 and the unofficial designation of "Mr. Helicopter." Since then, while honorary degrees and aviation medals have piled up in recognition of his work, he has introduced more than a dozen new helicopter models, including the world's first successful large transport.

Igor Sikorsky's own helicopters—and his is only one of nineteen makes now being produced in the United States alone—fly in nineteen countries, as far-flung as Formosa, the Belgian Congo, Argentina, Israel, and Australia, and are manufactured under license in Britain and France. They shuttle passengers, freight, and mail between the hearts of great cities and their airports and on short routes from city to city. In Belgium, Sabena uses them to link Brussels with such cities as Paris, Bonn, and Rotterdam. In British Columbia, they have strung power lines over the Rocky Mountains. Helicopters stand ready to taxi President Eisenhower from the White House lawn and carry Prince Philip on his frequent royal errands. They have landed yellow-fever vaccine in Costa Rican jungle clearings, suspended movie cameras over vast sets in Hollywood, threshed up a wind to blow the pecan crop out of the trees in Texas. Almost everywhere they dust crops, patrol forests, survey traffic, explore mining sites.

As a military craft, the whirlybird is not only performing old chores better but is dictating new tactics of war. The United States armed forces had an estimated 3,400 of them in 1957. The plane serves as aerial ambulance, supply truck, artillery spotter, wire layer, liaison and reconnaissance plane. It can spot and kill submarines or hover protectively alongside aircraft carriers to snatch fallen pilots from the waves. As a troop carrier the latest Sikorsky model can transport thirty-six fully equipped soldiers, and its nose opens wide to snuffle up jeeps and small field pieces. Both the U.S. Marines and the Army are counting on helicopters as the only practical assault craft of the atomic age.

The helicopter is the first aircraft that has saved more lives than it has taken. It has plucked the sick, the wounded, and the stranded from the desert, sinking ships, deep canyons, and mountain ledges all over the world. In the Korean war the helicopter was credited with the rescue or medical evacuation of more than 10,000 United Nations troops. Helicopters have also rescued earthquake survivors in Greece and flood victims in the United States, Mexico, Honduras, and the Netherlands. In August 1955, when floods swept parts of New England, thirteen helicopters from the Sikorsky factories near the flooded areas saved 475 men, women, and children in a single day.

Sikorsky is not only a name famed wherever men fly; it also stands for a proud new American clan. At last count there were forty-two Sikorskys in the United States, twenty-nine of them born with the name, thirteen of them Sikorskys by marriage, living from New York to California. Patriarch Igor and his wife, who have lived for years in a farmhouse in Easton, Connecticut, not far from the factory at nearby Stratford, have raised four sons: Sergei, now a sales representative for Sikorsky helicopters; Nicholas, who switched a few years ago from the violin to design engineering; Igor Jr., a lawyer; and George, a mathematician with International Business Machines. Although Sikorsky sees a good deal of his various relatives and also enjoys visits with such Russian expatriates as Countess Tolstoi and other old White Russian friends, many of his closest friends, such as the Charles Lindberghs, are people who simply share his passion for flight or his enthusiasms for an extraordinary range of interests and hobbies.

Through the years Sikorsky has filled his leisure at the piano, the telescope (he has a five-inch model in his home observatory), the camera, and in the seats of farm tractors. He putters with gadgets like small generators, loves to run his hands over a well-made machine, whether an aircraft engine or an industrial lathe. He has also written slim religious and philosophical volumes (*The Message of the Lord's Prayer, The Invisible Encounter*). With his Russian-born friends in the area, he was instrumental in building Stratford's Orthodox Church, whose interior is a small replica of the cathedral in Kiev. He loves heights, solitude, and contemplation, seeks them

*Sikorsky's first successful United States helicopter set new record in 1941.*

in mountain climbing and woodland walks as well as in aircraft. He pours energy into all his pursuits. On a commercial flight from New York to Los Angeles a few years ago, he amazed a traveling companion by spending all the time, except for meals and an hour's rest, engrossed for roughly equal intervals with the Bible, a volume of Plato, and a slide rule and work pad; he topped off the flight with a brisk two-mile walk before returning to his mathematics problem. One of Sikorsky's great passions is for volcanoes. He has flown thousands of miles to watch them erupt. Once a heavy smoker, he pledged that he would give up cigarets if he could light one from molten lava. He managed during an eruption of Mexico's famed Paricutin to make this habit-breaking gesture and stopped smoking for years; he now takes an occasional cigaret.

Volcano-chasing may well claim less of the older Sikorsky's leisure time, but he is still enchanted by the sheer love of flying and by contemplation of the wonders yet to come in the age of flight. For the helicopter, Sikorsky sees an unlimited ceiling of possibilities. The rise of jet transport planes with their enormous speeds, he believes, will turn such short routes as New York-to-Washington into helicopter runs. He thinks that the noisy jets will also tend to push airports farther away from cities, increasing the need for shuttling by helicopter. The Sikorsky plant is experimenting with turbine-powered helicopters, but a high-priority, long-range project, now emerging from scale model to the prototype stage, is the flying crane. It is Sikorsky's latest dream, a powerful helicopter that will lift cargo as an eagle carries a load in its claws. "Throughout history," he says, "all vehicles have been limited by weight and bulk, but the crane helicopter is limited only by the weight of the cargo it carries. Bulk doesn't matter. It can carry big ready-made houses, sections of bridges, hundred-foot lengths of pipe, and deliver them right where they are needed."

Sikorsky also looks to more distant horizons. In a 1930 interview he foresaw such developments as jet engines, pressurized cabins, scheduled daily flights to Europe, and helicopter commuter service. Today he predicts that passenger travel by rocket will become a reality within the lifetime of the present generation. "It can be said with complete assurance," he declares, "that traveling at several thousand miles per hour in the upper atmosphere can be reached within this period. . . ." Thanks to such pioneers as Sikorsky, the prospect seems less fantastic than the helicopter and the transoceanic Clipper appeared on that chilly day in 1919 when he sailed past the Statue of Liberty.

# Felix Frankfurter

*Felix Frankfurter*

*. . . We Americans are enlisted in a common enterprise—whatever our antecedents, whatever the creed we may avow or reject—the bold experiment of freedom. It is bold because it cannot be realized without the most difficult and persistent collaborative effort. It demands the continuous exercise of reason, and self-discipline of the highest order. This is so because it places ultimate faith for attaining the common good in the responsibility of the individual. . . . In this faith America was founded; to this faith have her poets and seers and statesmen and the unknown millions . . . devoted their lives.*

*by* A R C H I B A L D   M A C L E I S H

# A Tireless Quest for Justice

AMERICANS in the modern sense of that term have existed in the world for a very brief time, a few hundred years at most. Nevertheless, the world has been convinced for generations past that there is an American character, an American personality, which can be distinguished from the character, the personality, of other peoples. European travelers in the New World were certain of it as far back as Alexis de Tocqueville, and American travelers in Europe in more recent times have not only kept the certainty alive but vividly embroidered it. Nevertheless, neither De Tocqueville nor anyone else—not even the most articulate of Paris taxi drivers—has ever succeeded in putting the distinction into words.

The trouble is, of course, that European observers have looked for the American character in the wrong place. They have assumed that it would be found where the English character, for example, would be found: among the *echt* English, in the established families, the ancient pockets of the people. Whereas the fact is that the American character, in so far as it is distinguishable at all, is distinguishable not for reasons of habit or custom or a traditional mentality but precisely for the lack of habit, the lack of custom: for a mentality anything but fixed and settled. We may follow each other around like sheep through the supermarkets and the superhighways and the supersubdivisions but it is not by habit that we do it. The supermarket is a few years old and will be something else by next year, and as for the superhighways, they will be growing grass in half a generation. What Americans share is not the worn groove of predictability but an unpredictable restlessness: the love of something else, of something new. We have left the old world behind us. We are newcome men.

President Franklin Roosevelt put it into two wickedly perfect words when they wheeled him out in 1938 to address the Daughters of the American Revolution in their elegant new convention hall in Washington. The Daughters of the American Revolution, as every American knows, are worthy and respectable ladies who are able to trace their lineage back by one line or another to some ancestor who served the American cause in the 1770s. President Roosevelt was himself descended not only from soldiers of the Revolutionary armies but from even earlier Americans—the first settlers of the Hudson River valley. He met his audience, therefore, on the genealogical heights and spoke to them accordingly. "Fellow Immigrants!" he said, and paused and smiled.

The good ladies, some of them, took the words as a slight, and there was, no doubt, an edge of malice in the brightness of the smile that followed, but the words were apt. We are all immigrants, by whatever ship or plane, and it is in our quality as immigrants that our distinctive character as Americans exists. The immigrant mind is an unhitched mind, a runaway mind, a restless mind. It sees the world as possibility, not barrier. It rejects nothing on principle, tries anything in practice, takes the road that opens, builds and moves on, ends and begins again. It is a mind filled with the new-found world, in love with living.

All of which means that the American character should be most discernible in the newest Americans, in the men and women who are immigrants themselves. And of course it is. One of the most distinctively American minds in our generation is that of Felix Frankfurter, Associate Justice of the United States Supreme Court, whose father, a Viennese, visited the Chicago World's Fair in 1893, fell in love with the United States, established himself precariously as a sort of commission man in the city of New York, and sent for his wife and his four sons and two daughters to follow him. Mr. Justice Frankfurter, twelve years old when the journey was made in 1894, took no part, presumably, in the adventurous decision to become American. Indeed he seems to have remembered nothing of his Atlantic crossing but the unlikely name of the ship, the *Marsala,* the look of a plate of prunes, and his first taste of a banana. But he was an immigrant by conviction notwithstanding. He too fell in love with the new country—which meant, for him, the family flat on Seventh Street in Manhattan, Public School 25 on Fifth Street, the

*In the year of his arrival in America, aged twelve, Frankfurter sits with his younger brother, Paul.*

*Frankfurter stands with his hands on the shoulders of a City College of New York classmate in 1900.*

lovely Miss Pettigrew, daughter of the principal, who played the piano at assemblies, and the formidable teacher of his grade, a certain solid Miss Hogan who was given to underlining her instruction by sharp jabs to the jaw and who taught the little Austrian his English by so terrorizing the children of that predominantly German-speaking neighborhood that none of them dared speak to him in his native tongue. Felix Frankfurter was not a linguist then or later, but within four months of his arrival at Ellis Island and three months of his first encounter with Miss Hogan he had learned enough of the *lingua franca* of Fifth Street to catch up with the children of his own age and to go on through school and into City College of New York, from which he graduated at nineteen, third from the top of the class of 1902.

The milestones of that progress were an immigrant's milestones. There was the blue slip of untranslatable import with which the boy was sent home early on an autumn day in his first month—the slip which obviously meant that he had been expelled from school for some mysterious American crime but which turned out to say that Felix Frankfurter was a good boy and could have an hour off. There was the lovely lyric word which appeared again and again above the doors of the little shops of the neighborhood and which seemed to signify that a certain Herr Laundry was one of the principal proprietors of the New World but which, with time, took on a less romantic meaning. Most important of all, there was the newsstand and the daily paper. In Vienna you did not buy newspapers: you read them in a café and came home crammed with news. Here you could buy newspapers yourself, and in buying one you could glance at several and so come home with all the stories. Other American boys have made their way by selling newspapers. Felix Frankfurter made his by buying them, for once they were bought they had to be read and once they were read there was a new America to think about.

Moreover, as America grew larger the old country diminished, as it does with the true immigrant, until nothing remained of his mother's father, a miller in the little Bohemian town of Hungarische Osta, but a big beard and a menacing stick; and of his father's father, in Vienna, nothing but the beard. Somewhere in his mind there was a vague memory of inexplicable tears on his Viennese grandfather's face when the news had come of the death of Crown Prince Rudolph in the hunting lodge at Mayerling, but Austrian princes and Viennese tears were infinitely distant in this new landscape where there were actual things, immediate possibilities: such possibilities as the practice of the law.

Why the law, nobody knew, least of all Felix Frankfurter. There had been no lawyers in the miller's family and only one professional man of any kind in the family on either side, Dr. Solomon Frankfurter, a scholar of the University of Vienna. Nevertheless it was the law that loomed. Such things happen in a new country when you are young. You find yourself at beginnings everywhere and you know the right one by the way you turn, not by the way your parents turned before you.

It was an adventurous choice for Felix Frankfurter though not necessarily for others in his generation. Most young men who could afford it considered entering the law as a matter of course in those years. The difference was that Felix Frankfurter could not afford it.

He had made up his mind to go to the Harvard Law School because the law school at Harvard was the best in the country, then as now. But Harvard meant Cambridge, Massachusetts, and a room 225 miles away from home to live in and all the expenses that go with rooms far away from home, and he had no money. He was obliged, therefore, to add a year to the usual three postgraduate law school years to help earn his keep. He earned $1,200; and the $1,200, eked out by fees for tutoring his classmates, somehow got him through.

The combination of activities had, however, a consequence not foreseen. For, though Frankfurter did well in the school and had no difficulty in finding a place in a big New York law office, the private practice of the law seemed somehow insipid after everything that had gone before. It didn't feel like America—or like the America he had imagined. It didn't even feel like the law, for the law to this young lawyer was a human instrument, not a business tool. When, therefore, two months after his graduation from Harvard, he was offered an opportunity to serve on the staff of the United States District Attorney for the Southern District of New York, he jumped at it, never to return to the private practice of the law again.

The reason, at least in retrospect, is obvious. The three great passions of Frankfurter's life have always been the law, the United States of America, and people, and here he had all three together. He was practicing law at a level of significance and excitement which apprentice lawyers in big law offices never reach—trying cases of national importance against the leaders of the bar. He was serving the United States in a vigorous and effective campaign led by the President himself—Theodore Roosevelt's attack on "malefactors of great wealth" and "conscienceless corporations." And he was associated, in all this, with one of the noblest human beings of the time, the last of the great traditional American conservatives, Henry L. Stimson, who was later to serve his own Republican party as Secretary of War and Secretary of State and to return to Washington as Secretary of War under a Democratic president when World War II broke out.

Stimson was the simon-pure American idea in flesh and blood, a man of rigorous character and powerful intelligence who was at the same time warmly human: a conservative who understood, as most American conservatives once did understand, that what you conserve in a free country is freedom. He had accepted Theodore Roosevelt's invitation to head the office which would bear the brunt of the offensive against corporate corruption and lawlessness, regardless of the inevitable injury to his own practice, because he believed in individual freedom and opportunity. And he infused that office with a combination of courage, honesty, professional skill, and idealism which would have won the devotion of men less sensitive than Felix Frankfurter.

Frankfurter's association with the United States District Attorney for the Southern District of New York was not, perhaps, the greatest influence in his life but it left its indelible mark. Most young lawyers get over their idealism about the law in their first years in practice if not in law school itself. In my time in the Harvard Law School there was, as we used to put it, "no nonsense about justice"—and Frankfurter's day was only twelve years earlier than mine. Had he been born in the United States, had he taken the United States for granted, he might have said the same thing. But feeling as he did about the country, and practicing the kind of law he practiced under Stimson, he saw, and continued to see, the profession in a different perspective. He saw it as a means of making the future what the future ought to be: a means of realizing the New World dream which America still was to him even after the Socratic skepticism of the law school and the disillusionments of the New York of 1906.

The indictment of Charles W. Morse, the owner of the controlling interest in the Bank of North America, for embezzlement; the indictment of the New York Central Railroad for granting illegal rebates; and the indictment of officials of the American Sugar Refining Company for defrauding the Treasury by bribing customhouse functionaries to use improper weighing machines, were samples of the kind of case he was called on to try in the District Attorney's office. Indeed, the winning of the appeal in the Sugar

Frauds cases was Frankfurter's first great professional success. They were unsavory cases, but the fact that they could be fought and won, and the fact that a man like Stimson could be found to lead the fight, kept Frankfurter's faith intact. It grew stronger, not weaker. If it survived the revelation of frauds in New York, it also survived the revelation of somnolence and complacency in Washington.

In 1911 Stimson was made Secretary of War in the administration of President William Howard Taft and took his young assistant with him as Law Officer of the Bureau of Insular Affairs. That, at least, was Frankfurter's official title. Actually he served as a kind of general counsel to the Secretary. Taft's Washington was a place where nothing happened and happened as peacefully as possible—a kind of pleasant Indian summer after the heat of Theodore Roosevelt's day. But for Frankfurter the American excitement, the American urgency, remained. What *wasn't* happening without was canceled by furious happenings within. He and a group of young friends—Loring Christie, a future power in Canada; Lord Eustace Percy, who was to serve in a British cabinet; Robert G. Valentine, Commissioner of the American Indian Bureau—hired themselves an old, more or less tumble-down house on Nineteenth Street and proceeded to discuss, over luncheons and dinners and in the company of judges, senators, and philosophers, questions of such searching significance that Justice Oliver Wendell Holmes, after dining there, called the place, with mock solemnity, the House of Truth. It would more accurately have been called the House of Felicity, for it was Felix Frankfurter's invention. Wherever he sat, as they say of The MacGregor, was the head of the table. It was a habit, learned early, which he never lost.

Paradoxically—but perhaps not unforeseeably—it was this passion for human beings of intelligence, taken together with his passion for the public service of the United States and for the profession of the law, which provided Frankfurter's enemies, when he grew great enough to deserve them, with their principal weapon. In 1914, when he was still in his thirty-second year, Frankfurter was invited to join the faculty of the Harvard Law School and accepted. He

*Frankfurter presides over a discussion with his Harvard law students in the late 1930s.*

knew by then that the combination of people of intelligence on the one side, and professional devotion to the law on the other, which a great law school offers, was two-thirds, at least, of his desire. As for the other third, he probably guessed that his law school appointment would be no bar to further service of the Republic. Nor was it. During World War I he was in Washington, on leave from Harvard, for two years, ending up as chairman of the War Labor Policies Board and making in the process a number of new friendships, the most important of which, historically, was with a young Assistant Secretary of the Navy named Franklin Delano Roosevelt. Given the particular combination of Frankfurter's interests, this stance, with one foot in Harvard Law School and the other in the United States government, was bound to produce consequences, and it did. Frankfurter became a kind of inspired short circuit between the law school, which had previously considered itself a place which prepared young men for private practice, and the government of the United States, which had yet to realize how desperately it needed intelligence in its employees.

Frankfurter began luring young lawyers from private practice to public service under President Wilson, continued it for the benefit of the executive as well as the judicial branches of the government under the Republican Presidents who followed. Finally, under President Franklin Roosevelt, Frankfurter recruited dozens of young lawyers, most of whom did extremely well in Washington. A few, however, by virtue of their zestful genius, stirred up controversy enough so that President Roosevelt's enemies were tempted to make Frankfurter their principal target. He was a foreigner by birth. He was a Jew. And, best of all, he was a professor at Harvard. What could undermine public confidence in the President more effectively than the charge that he was permitting his friend Felix Frankfurter to infiltrate the government with radical Harvard students for dark and subversive purposes?

As it turned out, the terrifying picture frightened no one for very long except the newspaper columnists who peddled it. But there was enough talk and enough print so that memory of the charge stuck in the minds of the senators who questioned Frankfurter when he was nominated to the Supreme Court in 1939. His answer had an irony which was not noticed at the time. His mind, he said, had been shaped in these matters by two men. Henry L. Stimson had instilled in him "a high and fastidious sense of the law" and Theodore Roosevelt had "inspired a sense of civic duty within me as he did within so many young men." Theodore Roosevelt and Henry L. Stimson were, of course, Republicans.

If it struck Frankfurter as odd that a man should be abused for inspiring intelligent young lawyers to give up or postpone the rewards of private practice and accept instead the often ungrateful service of their country, he never said so. By 1939 he had grown accustomed to abuse. He had known it for twelve years' time. The story is simple but poignant and it still stirs passions. Twelve years before his elevation to the Supreme Court, when Frankfurter was in the middle of his rich career as a teacher and a student of the law, a criminal case which had been dragging through the courts of the Commonwealth of Massachusetts for six years reached a legal and dramatic crisis in the refusal of the trial judge, whose conduct of the case had been much criticized, to grant a new trial, even though new evidence had been discovered which seemed to show that the crime had been committed not by the defendants but by others. Appeal had been taken from this refusal to the Supreme Judicial Court of Massachusetts, friends were divided on the issue, newspapers took and changed sides, lawyers quarreled in public and in private, and, in the middle of all this, Frankfurter, who did not know the defendants and had no more than a law professor's concern with the questions that had been raised, decided he could no longer sit by in silence. He made an exhaustive and detailed examination of the voluminous record, concluded that there had been a miscarriage of justice, and published his analysis and his conclusions in the *Atlantic Monthly,* an influential general magazine with a relatively small but effective circulation throughout the country. Within a matter of hours he was one of the most violently controversial figures in the United States.

The case was the famous Sacco-Vanzetti case which began as the trial of two Italians, a fish peddler and a shoemaker, for the crime of murder and which ended, if it may be said to have ended, as the trial of a society for hysteria. The facts are familiar to all Americans. A brutal payroll murder had been committed in the Massachusetts town of South Braintree, not far from Boston. The suspicion of the local police had fallen on Nicola Sacco and Bartolomeo Vanzetti, who were known radicals and who were believed to need money for subversive purposes. They were arrested and brought to trial. The United States as a whole, and the Boston area in particular, was at the moment in the grip of one of those spasms of fear and suspicion which seem to be common and recurring American diseases, consequences perhaps—for the fear and suspicion is usually directed against foreigners—of the very fact to which President Roosevelt referred in his remarks to the Daughters of the American Revolution. Because we are all immigrants, and because it is as immigrants that we compose a nation, we long for inclusion in the stability of the nation, and we fear, above everything else, the more recent comer who may destroy that stability. It was these fears which were aroused by the panicky attempts of Attorney General Mitchell Palmer to round up the "Reds," his term for political dissidents of all kinds, after World War I. It was these same fears which Senator McCarthy and his associates exploited after World War II.

What Frankfurter's examination of the record in the Sacco-Vanzetti case suggested to him was that the two Italians were being tried for their political beliefs. That possibility, which seemed to him, indeed, a demonstrable fact, convinced him that he had no choice but to speak his mind. He was certainly not ignorant of the risks he ran. He knew that his foreign birth and his name would make him vulnerable to attack. He must have known that the Boston Bar, or some of its members, would regard it as highly improper for a professor in the Harvard Law School to discuss in public a case still before the courts, even though everyone else in Massachusetts was discussing it. Nevertheless he could not be still. He wrote his piece and published it—and the consequence was precisely what he must have foreseen.

His argument was persuasive then and is even more persuasive now. Its unstated assumptions were the great assumptions on which American law and American politics rest: the assumption that justice is the true end of law and that the right practice of the law can achieve it; the assumption that a free society need not tremble in fear before the radical and the revolutionary but can be true to itself and assure justice to every man in spite of his opinions; the assumption that even in a hysterical and frightened time, haunted by the suspicion of foreigners, a foreign-born American may speak for the American conscience without fear. But all this was brushed aside by the passions of the moment. Crackpots denounced Frankfurter as a foreigner and a Jew. His dismissal from Harvard was urgently demanded by numerous voices including, to Harvard's shame, the voices of some who had gone there. His name became synonymous with radicalism and even with bolshevism in the gutter press. But years later, when the Massachusetts Supreme Judicial Court had upheld the trial judges; and the Governor, supported by the moral authority of a distinguished committee appointed to advise him, had declined to intervene; and Sacco and Vanzetti had been executed; and the case had taken its sad and shameful place in history; it was in the great wave of protest against it and, above all, in the implicit affirmations of Frankfurter's article that the American conscience found its peace—such peace as it has found.

In 1932 the Governor of Massachusetts thought it politically possible to invite Frankfurter, even though his refusal was foreknown, to accept appointment to the Supreme Judicial Court whose rulings he had criticized. And twelve years after the *Atlantic* publication, when Frankfurter had accepted nomination to the Supreme Court of the United States and was before the Senate Committee on the Judiciary for confirmation, his intervention in the Sacco-Vanzetti case proved to be a strength rather than a weakness. The eleven witnesses against him were a curious little flock of men and women, including the national director of a "patriotic" organization, a Seneca Indian who thought the American Civil Liberties Union was a conspiracy to subvert the loyalty of the aborigines, and the ineffable Mrs. Elizabeth Dilling, a professional Red-hunter. These people depended heavily on the *Atlantic* piece of ammunition, and it was referred to again and again in the hearings. But as much because of his statement on the Sacco-Vanzetti case as for anything else, the committee voted unanimously to confirm Frankfurter's appointment; the Senate promptly followed.

What the fanatics of the various fringes were unable to understand, then or later, was not so much Felix Frankfurter as the American mentality itself. Those who insisted in 1927 that Professor Frankfurter must be a radical because he objected to the use of the judicial process in the trial of radicals—as well as those who announced fifteen years later that Justice Felix Frankfurter must be a reactionary because he upheld the right of the legislatures of the states to pass reactionary laws—were barking up the same tree at the same nonexistent cat. The American mind has never acknowledged the primacy of "doctrine" any more than the American language has accepted the meaningfulness of the word "intellectual" and for the same reason. The word "intellectual" implies that men are ticketed by their intellectual activities: that the dogma comes first and the man after; that the important thing about a human being is whether he wears the mental uniform of a conservative or a reactionary or a liberal or a radical. The Marxists of the 1930s who tried to domesticate "the intellectual" and the vigilantes of the 1950s who tried to lynch him had their trouble for their pains. "The intellec-

*Frankfurter with counsel Dean Acheson, later Secretary of State, listens to testimony at 1939 Senate hearings on confirmation of Supreme Court appointment.*

*Frankfurter at Oxford, in 1939, listening to Lady Astor at degree ceremony.*

tual" is not an American animal. The immigrant mind puts men first and things second and dogmas where they can find a place, and it won't reverse the order. When Frankfurter put a fair trial first and the philosophy of the defendants second he was acting as Americans have always hoped they acted. And when he reached judicial conclusions not on the basis of the philosophy of the New Deal—which, incidentally, never had one—but on the basis of the situation before him, he astonished no one but the doctrinaires. American judges have always thought they put the situation first.

In nothing, indeed, is Frankfurter more representative of the country he has made his own than in his dislike of doctrinaire positions. He is allergic, as most contemporary Americans are, to universal declarations of unalterable principles. He has never had any use for parties founded upon final and unarguable assumptions about the nature of the human animal, and neither have his fellow citizens. The principal reason why the Communist party failed so abjectly in the United States even in the darkest days of the Depression was not so much its brutality and cynicism, which were then skillfully concealed, as the American detestation of the smell of doctrine. That same detestation shows again and again in Frankfurter's expressions of his views. Government to him is not dogma in action. Government is an art—"one of the subtlest of the arts," as he has put it, "the art of making men live together in peace and with reasonable happiness."

That statement defines the task as most Americans would define it, though some of them might prefer another word than "art." It also defines the man who made it. To Frankfurter human life has always been the end, not of government alone, but of constitutions and laws as well. Societies exist not merely to exist but to provide the possibilities of man's fulfillment, and the limitations upon the governors, in a society such as ours, are and should be limitations to that end. It is this conviction which explains Frankfurter's eloquent concurring opinion in the Sweezy case, reversing a state court's decision against a university professor accused of concealing subversive associations—one of the three great reaffirmations of individual liberty which the Supreme Court handed down on June 17, 1957.

At the beginning of his judicial career there had been some talk of the possibility that Frankfurter, following Holmes, might make a distinction between permissible legislative interference with private enterprise in the economic field on the one hand and impermissible legislative interference with individual human rights on the other. In certain early opinions he had seemed to blur the distinction and to show himself disinclined to restrict the legislative branches of government in either area. But in the concurring opinion in the Sweezy case it was made explicitly clear that the freedom of the human mind is, under our Constitution, above and beyond the reach of legislatures and their committees as it is above and beyond any other agency of government. It is possible to surmise that the events of the late 1940s and early 1950s had demonstrated not only the

*Justice Frankfurter and his wife at their home in Cambridge, Massachusetts, 1939.*

wisdom but the necessity of Holmes's distinction. A government which would jeopardize the human ends for which it exists in order, somehow, to go on existing is a government on the verge of moral and political paralysis, and the great Justice had known it. That the present Court has made the same discovery and has stated it, through Chief Justice Earl Warren, in unambiguous words is a triumph for the American tradition which should have lasting consequences.

It is this fundamental, underlying belief in the value of human life, in the richness of its possibilities, in the sacredness of its hopes, which gives Frankfurter his peculiar quality. It explains his host of friends in all walks of life because it explains his eager interest in all forms of human activity. It explains his passion for talk, his impatience with dullness, his total incapacity for boredom. It explains his avid, hungry running and sniffing over the columns of newspapers and the pages of books like a small, agile dog following a confusion of scents in a wet field. It explains his warmth of personal affection, his love for his friends, his intense interest in the young, his trick of holding a listener, willing or not, above the elbow with nervous fingers which probe the bone.

Harold Laski, who never understood America very well because he had none of the immigrant's sense of a new world to be discovered, was made uncomfortable by Frankfurter's intensity. "He is always nervously restless," wrote Laski to Holmes early in Frankfurter's teaching career, "dashing here and there in a kind of creative fertility that drives me to despair. I don't find him able to sit down solidly to a single thing. He wastes the time that ought to be given to the permanent work that is in him in writing fine letters to antiquated New York lawyers with doubts about the Constitution. . . ."

Holmes, an elder immigrant of earlier generations, understood Frankfurter better and the real meaning of all this restlessness. It was not, as so many of his friends have thought and said, a mere excess of energy. It was, and is, an excess of love—an excess of the love of life—and it had a pattern which now, forty years after Laski's letter and many years after Laski's death, even his anxious eye might have noticed with approval. When Frankfurter's friends say, as they do, that the American whose disappearance from America would change it most is Felix Frankfurter, they mean that he has touched America most and known it best of any of them. He is more American than they or any man they know. He is more human.

*Helena Rubinstein*

# Helena Rubinstein

*I love beauty in all its aspects and find much of it to interest me in America. It is easy in America to envision a time when no woman will ever look old, regardless of her age—indeed, that time is practically here right now.*

*There is a spirit of hopefulness and youth in America which is most stimulating to me. Here one does not live in the past, but in the pulsating present and exciting future. Nothing is impossible in America—and since that is my personal credo, I feel very much at home here.*

*by* RICHARD CARTER

# High Priestess of American Beauty

EXCEPT for a very few who have inherited their wealth or have married it, the richest woman in America is Helena Rubinstein, who is now worth at least a hundred million dollars, every penny of which she has earned herself. At an age hardly less than eighty the tiny, Polish-born Madame Rubinstein continues to work seven days and seven nights a week, fifty-two weeks a year, augmenting the wealth and fame she has won through services rendered to the morale of other women around the world and particularly in the United States.

These services are considerable. If the average American woman now weighs 128 pounds instead of the 132 of thirty years ago; if she carries her five feet four inches so erectly and so gracefully that her trim waist seems even more slender than it is; if she strides

59

freely, smiles whitely, gazes luminously from beneath delicately shadowed lids and artfully penciled brows; if her smooth cheeks glow ever so slightly and her hair shines ever so brightly; if, in sum, she has become more of a delight, compliment, and challenge to her male companions, Helena Rubinstein is entitled to a good deal of the credit for the achievement.

Madame Rubinstein is, of course, the world's most celebrated beauty culturist. As long ago as 1915 she took leadership in persuading United States women that heredity is not the sole source of physical charm. Under Madame Rubinstein's warm but imperious prodding they learned that, by disciplining the body and utilizing the unguents of therapy and artifice purchasable at better shops, they could make the most of their natural endowments. In the process, the entire beauty business emerged from its old rice-powder, rose-water, and cold-cream phase and developed into a two-billion-dollar-a-year industry.

To say that Madame Rubinstein is a beauty culturist means only that she is a manufacturer and seller of cosmetics and an operator of beauty salons. But she has embellished her trade with pomp so splendiferous and authority so awesome that, in her hands, it seems hardly to be a trade at all and attains the status of an evangelical ministry of the skin.

Aside from an invincible ambition, Madame Rubinstein's chief asset is an almost occult faculty for conveying the impression that, if she stocks a balm, it must be straight from Gilead. Undoubtedly the impression is reinforced by Madame's assiduous cultivation of her own public personality as a high priestess and demi-doctor of glamor who cares intensely and constantly about the futures of the faces and figures on which her preparations are daubed.

Her chunky but well-organized physique is invariably dressed in splendor (usually by Balenciaga) and festooned with jewels selected from her million-dollar assortment. In such trappings and moving at her characteristic steady half-trot, she sets a breakneck pace for her competition. To oversee her vast holdings she spends at least half the year traveling, which gives her numerous opportunities to stage portentous arrivals and departures in the world's great cities, her dark eyes snapping with the excitement of discovery and acquisition—a new hormone to freshen the skin, a new painting added to her famous collection of modern art, a new fashion to be analyzed, a new anecdote to be told in a softly accented contralto.

Madame now employs thirty thousand persons in factories, laboratories, and salons in the United States, Canada, Mexico, Colombia, Brazil, Argentina, Chile, England, Ireland, France, Switzerland, Germany, Italy, Spain, South Africa, Australia, and New Zealand. In 1957 total sales of sixty million dollars were reported by her United States corporation and its various overseas affiliates.

Information of this kind has to be pried out of Madame Rubinstein. Although she takes great pleasure in her fortune and nurtures it fondly, she much prefers to discuss hard work ("I am nothing but a slave to work") and science ("I have always been deeply involved in science"), which she considers to be the secrets of her success.

"I would have been a physician," she says, exuding regret, "but when I went to the University of Zurich for my medical training I found that I could not stand the sights and smells. Blood! I used to faint every time I went into the operating room."

She had gone to Zurich at the age of about eighteen from her childhood home in Krakow, Poland, where she was born in a year that she refuses to divulge. After her return from Zurich her father, an importer in Krakow, packed her off to Australia to visit relatives. She stayed for several years, first as an unhappy guest on her uncle's sheep ranch near Coleraine, in Victoria, and next as a governess in Queensland. She was an energetic figurine of a girl with piercing dark eyes and a creamy, city-bred skin that contrasted spectacularly with the wind-burned complexions of the Australian women.

It was by exploiting this contrast that she first began to develop her ability to work wonders with feminine morale. It started when envious Queensland girls inquired about her fair skin and were told to their amazement that the secret came in a jar. It was called Valaze Cream, Helena revealed, and it was blended by a physician in Krakow from the bark of a Carpathian tree and herbs of miraculous efficacy. The Queensland girls clamored for the substance and Miss Rubinstein obliged, charging four shillings a jar and profiting from each new shipment sent from Poland. There the happy physician soon set up his own jar factory.

A less formidable woman might have been content to ride along on the commercial momentum provided by her own rosy cheeks and her ability to obtain Valaze Cream, but young Helena Rubinstein was shrewd enough to seek knowledge with which to lend substance to her new authority.

"I studied the whole time," she says. "I read myself sick. I became an expert. And every penny I got I saved and sent for more cream."

In 1904 Miss Rubinstein expanded to London, partly because it was a logical next step and partly because her fiancé, an American newspaperman named Edward W. Titus, had just been transferred there from Melbourne.

The London performance was more sophisticated. Instead of operating in a modest shop, Miss Rubinstein rented Lord Salisbury's twenty-room mansion in Mayfair and, instead of purveying Valaze Cream to any kitchen menial who happened to have faith and four shillings, she catered to the carriage trade. With adroit nudges from elegant advertisements written by Edward Titus, free-spending peeresses began flocking to the new Maison de Beauté.

The London opening, however, did not mean closing down the Australian branch of the Rubinstein business. Though thousands of miles away, Madame Rubinstein, as she now became known, continued to superintend the Australian installation, demanding and receiving frequent progress reports. Before long she had opened salons in Paris and in other cities of Europe.

In the midst of all this she also found time to marry Titus and to bear him two sons, both of whom became executives of her empire. Her recollections of Titus are wry. "He was an intellectual, my American husband," she says, "and he collected artistic people. They overran my house."

While the husband collected the people, the wife collected

*Young Helena was photographed in a wide-brimmed hat before she left Poland for Australia.*

their works. The long, successful business day was insufficient stimulation for Madame. In her spare time, instead of seeking conventional recreation, she acquired paintings at bargain rates. Dozens of Picassos, Modiglianis, Rouaults, Renoirs fell into her hands to be hung on the walls of her various homes or stored in closets and cellars. Even this was not enough. She began collecting sculpture, primitive carvings, silver spoons, old silks, dolls, first editions, milk glass, jewels, antique furniture, pink opaline, masks, and miniatures. Nobody, including Madame Rubinstein, knows how much she has collected or where it all is or how much it is worth. Experts say that her collection of modern art, to which she still adds, is one of the world's largest, most ill-assorted, and most valuable.

When war broke out in 1914, Edward Titus wanted to return to the United States. After getting her European affairs in impregnable order and tightening the leash on Australia, Madame set sail. Arriving in New York, where she was entirely unknown, she sensed that the American cliché, "Land of Opportunity," had all the truth of most clichés. What had gone before had been only a rehearsal for what was to come.

If she had known all about American history and American

sociology and if she had combined this mass of knowledge with miraculous powers of prophecy, Helena Rubinstein could scarcely have selected a more propitious time to establish herself in the United States. The American public—particularly its female component—was about to be propelled into an era in which it would be most receptive to her products and her methods.

For at least two generations before this winter of 1914–15, America's more upright elements had been cultivating forms of social respectability designed to efface the memory of a raucous, brawling, pioneering past. Evoking the ethics of Puritanism and embracing the rigors of Victorianism, right-thinking American men turned their ramrod backs on the frivolous and moved through life with uncomfortable collars, high shoes, and frozen frowns. American women went in for a good deal of Victorian twittering and swooning and displayed such dubious insignia of their sex as the briefly fashionable bustle. But their most evident quality was a sanctimonious kind of self-denial known at the time as "modesty."

Modesty decreed, among other things, that a girl with a plain face had to go through life that way. Facial paint was condemned as the weapon of a hussy. A respectable woman might use a little rice powder, or even a dab of cold cream, but was strictly forbidden to try anything that might do her appearance any lasting good.

It is, of course, inconceivable that a people as exuberant as the Americans could have long enjoyed customs of such inanity. Puritanism and Victorianism began to crumble with the first reverberations of World War I. With America's entry into that war, the demolition process was completed. Excusing themselves to their disapproving elders on the grounds that shackles were inappropriate equipment in an age of tension and dislocation, American women began to take up cigaret smoking, face painting, and other affectations that had so recently been considered forms of depravity. At the same time, they redoubled their efforts to win the right to vote and soon won it.

For Madame Rubinstein and the industry which she was now to lead, this atmosphere of liberation was ideal. It still is. It is estimated that the per-capita annual expenditure on cosmetics of the over fifty-six million American women above eighteen is about $23, and the industry's volume increases steadily, not only because the population increases steadily, but because Madame Rubinstein and her competitors are forever introducing enticing new products that few American girls are able to pass up.

What was considered immodest artifice in 1914 is now considered common sense. Every American girl in her right mind makes herself as attractive as possible, an effort that involves purchase of chic clothes but is concentrated on the well-groomed face and well-molded figure around which the chic is assembled. American men, far from disapproving such attention to matters of vanity, applaud it. More than that, they boast about it.

In discussing the role she has played in altering the face of her adopted nation, Madame Rubinstein likes to recall her arrival in New York. With the same chuckle that occasionally wells out of her as she trots through one of her salons, she says of her arrival, "It was a cold day. All the American women had purple noses and gray lips. And their faces were chalk-white from terrible powder. I recognized that the United States could be my life's work."

In 1915 she opened her first Maison de Beauté on East Forty-ninth Street in New York. An advertisement featured an etching of Madame and informed the magazine's readers that "Queens, princesses, celebrated artists, and leaders of high society all acknowledge Mme. Helena Rubinstein to be the World's Greatest Beauty Culturist."

Since another famous purveyor of beauty products, Elizabeth Arden, had already convinced an impressive fraction of the queens, princesses, celebrated artists, and leaders of high society resident in the United States that *she* was the World's Greatest Beauty Culturist, the Rubinstein manifesto touched off a vendetta that flames to this day. Although Madame Rubinstein's United States business was estimated in a recent year to be twice as big as Miss Arden's in total volume, Madame Rubinstein is less gratified by this than by raids she has made on Arden personnel over the years. Her outstanding feat

*In 1915, at the time of her arrival in America, she looked poised and confident after successes in Melbourne and London.*

of that kind came in 1939 when, retaliating for the loss of her general manager to Miss Arden, she triumphantly announced that she had hired Miss Arden's ex-husband to fill the position.

At the outset, partly because her rival was so firmly entrenched as society's beautician, Madame Rubinstein decided to emphasize glamor in the United States as a therapeutic necessity as well as a matter of high fashion. Accordingly she reduced the stress on queens and princesses and invoked science. In the summer of 1915 a Rubinstein advertisement was the first ever to offer a scientific reason why women should hasten to purchase a skin preparation.

"Sunlight," said the ad, "is composed of rays of different colors, and amongst these are blue rays and violet rays." Madame's "new wonderful preparation" would "debar" these rays from "staining or browning the skin. . . ."

"They used to come to my salon surreptitiously," she recalls nostalgically, "and tell only their closest friends that it was I who had made their complexions so lovely."

The clandestine phase lasted only until 1917, as the resultant female emancipation took on the aspects of a stampede. Madame realized that millions of women were waiting, pale-cheeked, for her leadership. She opened new salons in Washington, Chicago, Boston, and Toronto, and, with her sister Manka to help her, she shuttled from coast to coast demonstrating her wares to awed customers in the best department stores of the largest cities. One Rubinstein fan who watched an early demonstration in Boston remembered it years later: "Madame had on a very décolleté tomato-colored dress and a great deal of jewelry. The women were popeyed. They bought everything."

After hours, before returning to her hotel to check the latest reports from her salons and factories, Madame tutored the shop clerks in sales methods. Even though American women were beginning to buy rouge, they were still tending to use only one cream—cold cream—and by Madame Rubinstein's standards were badly in need of re-education. The shopgirls were therefore taught to be teachers, a Rubinstein innovation that has since become a tradition.

Madame has not found it necessary to alter this approach in any important particular during all the years that have elapsed since she became firmly established as American Beauty Expert Number One. The "Paris Beauty Courses" which her thirty traveling demonstrators stage in department stores are much like the virtuoso performance with which Madame conquered her Boston audience years ago.

Not long ago, for example, Madame's gorgeously tailored niece, Mala Rubinstein, superintended a week of demonstrations in a San Antonio, Texas, store. Each session lasted two hours and was attended by fifty eager women, each of whom spent two dollars for the privilege. Upon arrival the women were stationed at vanity tables equipped with well-illuminated mirrors and were given kits containing several cosmetics, cotton, facial tissue, gauze, plastic bibs, heartening literature ("Your purchase of Helena Rubinstein's Paris Beauty Course is the beginning of a truly beautifying experience"), and a "Beauty Guide" in which a Rubinstein assistant checked off prescriptions for exercise, diet, and the types and shades of cosmetics likely to have the most salubrious effect in the specific case.

Having learned how, when, and why to apply the products that are to be sold to her, the customer must then decide which to buy. The possibilities are dizzying. The Rubinstein armamentarium consists of 466 strikingly packaged items, each representing months or years of thought and experimentation by Madame (who spends much of her time in the laboratory getting her hands all gooey) and her technical assistants.

If, as Madame hopes will frequently be the case, the customer wants to pamper herself with beauty aids containing a couple of female hormones, compelling reasons will exist for purchasing Estrogenic Hormone Cream with Progesterone (for the face), Estrogenic Hormone Oil (for the throat), Silk-Tone Foundation Special with Estrogenic Hormones (as a make-up base), and Young Touch Hand Lotion with Estrogenic Hormones.

Some customers forego hormones because they have learned

to swear by the results achievable with water lily buds, wine, and fermented milk, which are among the key ingredients of Skin Dew. Other preparations are brewed from such other staples of the medieval sorcerer as cucumber juice, honey, Irish moss, Italian parsley, and seaweed. The original bark-and-herb cream with which Madame lubricated billions of Australian wrinkles is now known as Wake-up Cream, and Madame continues to use it herself. But it no longer sells very well. "It isn't expensive enough," she says. "People won't buy it when they can buy something else for more money."

This lucrative truth is demonstrated daily not only at drug and department-store counters but in Madame's own salons. Although the salons make little money, they are fundamental to the Rubinstein way of doing things: they are cathedrals of cosmetology, and a woman who has been to one is likely to remain a true believer forever. The main attraction is a queenly experience known as The Day

*In her laboratory with chemist Dr. Julius Wetterhahn, Madame examines a batch of camomile flowers, an important ingredient of her lotions.*

of Beauty. As one refreshed young woman reported recently after undergoing the seven-hour, $35 renovation in the New York salon, "It would make a sybarite out of a fishwife."

Once a fad of New Yorkers, Parisians, and other cosmopolitan clients, The Day of Beauty has become a major attraction for American women across the country, many of whom now use it as an excuse for an annual trip to Madame Rubinstein's headquarters. The Day of Beauty is a day of tender massage, mild exercise, luxurious ablution in scented foam, voices crooning flattery and warning gently of pitiable consequences should the new regimen not be continued. It is an entire day of peach satin pillows, fragrant oils, and titillating astringents. It includes a medical examination by a lady doctor and the creation of a coiffure so distinctive that no other hairdresser can figure it out and the woman has no choice but to return to the salon next time she needs a haircut.

For several years a high point of this glorious overhaul was a fantastically elaborate lunch of vegetarian delicacies which bore such names as "Emeralds in Sunlight" and "Gauguin Sunburst." "The first year I lost fifty thousand dollars on those luncheons," Madame reminisces. "The second year I lost thirty and the third year ten. It was very depressing. I like to help people to be healthy and have fine skins, but I couldn't continue to charge only $1.65 for those luncheons when they cost me three or four dollars."

The lunches were abandoned. If today's customer is overweight, she is urged to eat a salad, which is sent from a nearby food shop. Otherwise, the shop sends up a sandwich and coffee.

Madame almost enjoys recalling the losses she suffered from the lunches, possibly because her life has otherwise been bereft of financial failure, to use an understatement. The sheer novelty of the lunch debacle appears to amuse her in retrospect—not, however, that she is anxious for more such novelties. In the same spirit of not spending money unnecessarily, Madame Rubinstein is ruthless about absenteeism, clock watching, needless purchases, misuse of the company's telephonic facilities, and other forms of commercial waste. Also, she drives a hard bargain. One of her former associates once observed, "If somebody offered Rubinstein a package of chewing gum for a nickel she would say 'Too much' in the hope that it was the only package of gum in the world that could be bought for four cents."

Madame's employees who are willing to give nearly as much devotion to their work as Madame does can count on remaining with her as long as they like. For personnel in responsible jobs, devotion means availability for overtime work every day of the week and, on short notice, any night. To stay home with an ailment so trivial as a cold or a sick headache is to betray a lack of will power tinged with disloyalty. Madame cannot understand why everybody else is not as single-minded about the business as she is, and the thought is a wound. "People just don't like to work any more," she says.

Still her business prospers, and on the side Madame supplements her large income with only slightly smaller sums derived from real estate investments and the stock market. Madame's greatest stock coup came during the Depression and is still recalled with shudders by the mighty Wall Street firm of Lehman Brothers. In 1928 the great banking house decided that it would be a splendid idea to buy out Madame and put her label on a low-priced line of cosmetics. After much hesitation she sold two thirds of her Western Hemisphere business for $7,300,000 in cash, retaining full ownership of the European and Australian affiliates. For about a year her sufferings increased as she watched the Lehmans, as she describes it, "selling my creams in grocery stores." At last she was unable to restrain herself from informing the stockholders that ruination was afoot. Her circular letters to this effect were particularly irksome to the new management because in the interim the stock market had crashed. The shares plummeted. When they had fallen from $70 to $3, Madame bought back a controlling interest in the firm for $1,500,000, retaining a clear profit of $5,800,000.

Busy with her investments and with her salons and factories and sales figures and personnel problems and new products and advertising campaigns and transoceanic voyages and interviews and collections of art, Madame was not surprised to find that she and

Edward Titus had drifted apart. She divorced him in 1937. The following year she married Prince Artchil Gourielli-Tchkonia, an amiable Georgian expatriate in whose honor she founded the Gourielli line of men's toiletries.

Like everybody else associated with Madame, the prince regarded her with profound amazement. Unlike many others, however, he was not cowed. This was emphasized during the early days of their marriage when he took a chisel and gouged chips out of the priceless mother-of-pearl bedstead which once had belonged to the Duc de Montpensier and now adorned Madame's Paris boudoir. The bed, he said, looked too perfect. The marriage was successful and lasted until the prince's death in 1955.

Madame continues to use the three-floor, twenty-six-room penthouse on New York's Park Avenue, the mansion in Greenwich, Connecticut, the apartment on Quai de Béthune in Paris, and the villas at Combs-la-Ville and Grasse. Park Avenue is the home base. She resides there about half the year and travels the rest of the time, ransacking the world for additions to her art collection and intermittently breathing down the necks of those who manage her foreign enterprises.

At intervals it has occurred to her to withdraw from the frenzied competition of the American cosmetic industry. "In the Old World," she says, "you make one good product and you are set for five generations." Her desire for such tranquillity always subsides quickly, just as it did the time she snatched her firm back from Lehman Brothers. Her whole life is business—the more hectic the better— and no business gratifies her like the business she can wage in America. "Every time I return to America from no matter what country, I get a new thrill and feel stimulated and inspired," she says.

In 1953, as if to encourage such feelings elsewhere in the world, she paid twenty Italian painters from $100 to $300 each, depending on their previously established market price, for paintings depicting the United States. Since all but two of the artists had never seen the United States, the results were striking. Aldo Pagliacci, who likes to paint burning churches, showed St. Patrick's Cathedral in New York on fire. Nino Caffe, who likes to paint priests, showed priests playing baseball. Colombotto Rooso showed the Rocky Mountains rising out of the sea, and Leonardo Cremonini committed an abstraction entitled "Nebraska." Before shipping the canvases back to Park Avenue to age and gain value, Madame exhibited them at Rome's exclusive L'Obelisco gallery—and incidentally got reams of publicity.

On such occasions Madame is accused of turning art to commercial purposes. Her critics apparently feel that it would be more appropriate for her to buy her paintings quietly and, when exhibiting them, contrive to attract less attention to herself and more to the exhibition. These sentiments are not widely endorsed in the art world, which has few patrons as active as she.

In this field, as in many other nonbusiness ones, Madame Rubinstein's benefactions are almost as complex as her business activities. In addition to helping young, unknown artists with grants and with purchases of their works she has, for instance, given $250,000 to endow a new art pavilion in Tel Aviv and encourage the exchange of Israeli and United States artists. And perhaps to prove that her preoccupation with art has not made her slight her first love, science, she also recently endowed a chair of chemistry at Brandeis University in Massachusetts. Another of her enduring concerns is with aiding children, and here her money and energies have gone into everything from helping to stock hospitals with blood for needy children to assisting boys' clubs and community centers in slum areas.

"Just because I have money does not mean that I am not helping people," says Madame. "I cannot help making money."

She utters that last truth woefully, like someone describing his inability to hold a job. But when asked why she does not take a day off once in a while, she looks almost frightened. She clenches her tiny fists, bats her eyes, shakes her head slowly from side to side, and whispers, "I was born to work."

*Dalip Saund*

# Dalip Saund

*As a student in India, all that I knew about America was what I read in the British textbooks. I knew all about George III but was kept in ignorance concerning one of the greatest historical events of all times. I refer to the American Revolution—an incident which, in my opinion, has done more to bring joy and dignity to the lives of men than anything before or since in the annals of man.*

*by* R O B E R T   W.   G L A S G O W

# *From Chhajalwadi to the United States Congress*

IN the social and political hierarchy of Washington, new members of the lower house of Congress are usually far less conspicuous than the United States capital's second-string bureaucrats or many of the tourists for whom they are often mistaken. Among these freshman arrivals in the House of Representatives in 1957 was a dark-complexioned man from southern California's Twenty-ninth District. As he conscientiously went about his homework of studying new legislation and attending committee meetings, it soon became apparent that he would not long share the other newcomers' anonymity.

He stood out because of his name, Dalip Singh Saund, because he was a Hindu born in the Punjab, and because he was the first Asian immigrant ever elected to the United States Congress. The manner of his election gave him further distinction: running as a Democratic party candidate in a traditionally Republican party district in a year of a landslide Republican presidential victory, Saund had won a nationally publicized race against the famous, glamorous aviatrix, Jacqueline Cochran.

Saund's congressional colleagues quickly realized that he was not going to be content to rest on the publicity he had gained from his unusual background and his spectacular election victory. When he was given an almost unprecedented honor for a freshman, appointment to the powerful House Foreign Affairs Committee, he made effective use of it. Not long afterward he embarked on an extensive tour of Asia as a one-man subcommittee to help improve relations between the United States and Asia—and also as a one-man symbol of the workings of United States democracy.

High point of Dalip Saund's six-thousand-mile trip through his native India was his return after thirty-seven years to his native village of Chhajalwadi in the Punjab. There, to the piping of flutes, the beat of drums, and the cheers of flower-bearing villagers, he held a tearful reunion with a sister and brother who had stayed at home. And there, as he had in scores of other Indian towns, he stood up before a huge crowd to explain his feelings about India and America.

In such speeches Saund did not ignore unpleasant aspects of American life as he had lived it. "I explained," he said recently, "that in the earlier years the people of California had not wanted Chinese, Japanese, or Indians in their communities—at least they did not want them as equals. I recalled that there had been laws denying some of us citizenship and prohibiting others from owning land for farming purposes. I made it clear that we had been severely discriminated against.

"But," he adds, "I also explained that these abuses are largely in the past, that all of this has changed since World War II. I cited my own case as an illustration of how much things had changed. I emphasized that one of the remarkable things about a democracy is that it does permit people to change and to make changes. I noted that the fact I was an Indian and had fought my way up, instead of working against me in my campaign for Congress, had worked for me. The minorities—such as Negroes, Mexican-Americans, and Indians—constituted a very small fraction of the voters in my district, so that it took far more than the minority vote to put me in office. This could not have happened ten years ago."

Chhajalwadi, Saund's birthplace, is near the city of Amritsar and about sixteen miles from what is now the Pakistan border. He was born there on September 20, 1899, the son of a well-to-do family of government contractors, builders of canals and railroads. They were Sikhs, members of a reformed Hindu sect which, among other things, rejects the idea of caste. Young Saund, following grammar and high school in Amritsar, attended and was graduated from the Sikh college there.

Though he never met or saw Gandhi, Saund soon came to know the writings of this great man. He knew little about the U.S.A. until World War I, when he began to read stories in Indian newspapers about Woodrow Wilson, his Fourteen Points, and his slogan "Make the World Safe for Democracy." When one of Wilson's speeches referred to another American statesman, Abraham Lincoln, Saund made an overnight trip to the University of Punjab to borrow books about Lincoln.

Saund graduated from college in 1919, and his parents prepared to line up a career in Britain's Indian Civil Service for him. As a Gandhi disciple and a fervent Indian nationalist, Saund turned down the proposal, as his means of boycotting the British government. Instead, he decided his place was in private business. He had noticed that almost all canned foods in India were either British or American and decided that there probably would be good opportunities in an Indian canning industry. Saund had heard that the University of California at Berkeley was an outstanding place to prepare for such a career. This, plus his old interest in Wilson and Lincoln, led him to leave for the United States in 1920.

Saund came to the United States by way of London, where he stayed only two or three weeks, unable to enjoy the customary sights because of his impatience to get to America. He entered his new country through the once-traditional gateway for millions of immigrants: Ellis Island in New York Harbor. There the long lines of pushing and shoving people waiting to be processed were a momentarily dismaying experience. "I'll never forget," he says, "there was a long table with food on it and there were immigrants from everywhere sitting at this table, eating. I had been brought up to be polite and I was shocked at the way these people were grabbing food from each other's plates."

On the long train trip from New York to California he was equally bewildered by the stares of fellow passengers and the strange foods. "I wore a turban and everybody just looked at me," he recalls. "The food was new to me, so I mostly lived on milk." In San Francisco at first things were not much better. "I went to a Traveler's Aid station in the ferry building and explained to them I wanted to go to Berkeley. For some reason they sent me to a downtown mission where I was given a small room. I soon found the bed full of bedbugs so I tried to sleep on the floor. I was alone and I didn't know where I was. It was the most terrible night I ever spent."

The following morning Saund found his way to Berkeley and the University of California. At the university he was told that there were about eighty Indian students on the campus and a Hindu Students' Association which had its own residence clubhouse.

Established in the clubhouse, Saund promptly enrolled in some agricultural courses. At the same time he learned that if he were to take courses in mathematics, it would be fairly easy for him to obtain a master's degree. This he did, subsequently going on to take his doctorate in mathematics. By the end of his first year in Berkeley the Ellis Island dining table had become only a wry recollection. Saund had made many American friends and was appearing often before the Young Men's Christian Association, church and student groups to talk about India.

To this day Saund is not quite sure when he abandoned the idea of getting into the canning business. But during the summer following his first year at Berkeley he tried his hand at it by taking

*Young Saund in the United States wore Sikh turban for portrait painted by his brother-in-law, Emile Kosa, Jr.*

a job at a California Packing Corporation plant in nearby Emory-ville. He was placed in charge of the syrup department. Near the end of the summer the plant superintendent invited Saund to his home for dinner. Saund recalls the evening well.

"After we had dinner this man started asking me questions as to what I was going to do in life. I was so confused and undecided at the time that I told him that I didn't know whether to write a history of India, to be a teacher, to go back to India and be a political fighter, or to go into the canning business. A few days later he told me, 'Young man, you talked yourself out of a job the other night. I had decided to offer you the job as assistant plant superintendent. But I wasn't interested in training a man who might quit the next day to write a history of India.' "

Though he still did not know what his ultimate plans were, Saund continued to study at the university and to work in canning plants during the summers to finance his education. Reading French and German mathematics texts gave him considerable difficulty, but he finally got his Doctor of Philosophy degree. (Title of his thesis: "On Functions Associated with the Elliptic Cylinder in Harmonic Analysis.") He promptly received offers of teaching jobs from a college in Indiana and an engineering school in Pennsylvania. Still undecided, he turned them down.

But already forming in his mind was the decision that was to shape the rest of his life. It stemmed indirectly from his devout observance of his religion. "I used to go to a Sikh temple in Stockton to celebrate religious days," he recalls, "and would meet other Hindus who had immigrated to California. Some who couldn't even read and write were driving big Cadillacs. I asked where they made their money and was told that they were farmers from the Imperial Valley. So I decided to go down there and make money, too."

The Imperial Valley is a vast former desert area in the extreme southern section of California which has been turned into a great natural hothouse through irrigation. Fortunes are constantly being made—and, as Saund soon learned, lost—in such crops as cotton and in the highly speculative business of growing carrots, lettuce, and other greens for the winter markets in cities of the eastern United States.

Saund went to the Imperial Valley in the fall of 1925 and was given a job by a Hindu farmer as foreman of a cotton-picking gang. "That's about the only use I ever made of my mathematics," he says. "I checked the weights of the pickers' cotton bags and I made good money—$17 or $18 a day—and was soon able to save up enough to lease a piece of land of my own." He brought in a fine lettuce crop. But so, it seemed, did everyone else that year.

"There was just too much lettuce. I lost everything," he says. Nevertheless, he remained in the Imperial Valley, trying to farm on leased land. "I was getting by, that was all," says Saund.

Despite the hard work of farming, Saund had not given up his intellectual interests. In 1927, in fact, he was inspired to start work on the book about India which he had long thought of writing. His inspiration came from what he considered a grossly unfair portrait of his country in a sensational best seller of the time, Katherine

Mayo's *Mother India*. Incensed, as were most of his countrymen, by what he considered the book's exaggerations of India's backwardness, Saund began to write a rebuttal called *My Mother India*.

The next year Saund briefly left the valley to go up to Los Angeles and work intensively on his book. One evening after he had spoken before a meeting of the First Unitarian Society in Hollywood, a tall American came up and invited Saund to visit him at home. Saund politely declined but later bumped into the same man —Emil Kosa Jr., a young artist—in a cafeteria. Again Kosa invited Saund to visit his home. This time Saund accepted.

Kosa's father was a well-established artist and the family had a pleasant home on Sunset Boulevard. There Saund met other members of the family, including Emil's pretty, blond nineteen-year-old sister, Marian, who was a student at the University of California at Los Angeles. Saund and the Kosas took to each other at once. Mrs. Kosa was interested in international relations and loved to listen to young Saund's views. Marian was fascinated by Saund's ability to recite the English poets and by his own English translations of Indian poetry. The two were married within six months after their first meeting.

With his bride Saund returned to the Imperial Valley. In Westmoreland he renewed his farming efforts. His book, which appeared in 1930, pleased his fellow Hindu nationalists but was not a commercial success. He managed to make a living on his farm during the early depression years, then in 1934 hit what looked to him like the jack pot: he made about $7,000 from an alfalfa crop. "Then I plunged into alfalfa," Saund sadly recalls, "and the price went to nothing. I was broke again.

"By this time I had three children and found myself owing about $10,000. My prospects were terrible. Several of my neighbors filed bankruptcy proceedings. The fertilizer and seed companies and my other creditors advised me to do the same. I was very sensitive about bankruptcy. My father's people had a custom that when a man takes out bankruptcy, he must set a kerosene lamp burning in his window in the daytime as a mark of his shame. If I had filed for bankruptcy I would have felt just as if I had that lantern in my window."

Some creditors got judgments against Saund, but he did not file for bankruptcy and continued to pay a little at a time on his debts. After several years he was at last in the clear. As World War II came along, creating new demand for foodstuffs, he began to prosper.

Though the 1930s were hard years for Saund, there were pleasant aspects. He began to participate in community life—as a member of service clubs, a worker and leader in charity fund drives. He also became interested in politics and joined various Democratic party organizations.

But there was a rankling obstacle. Saund could not vote. He was not a citizen and could not become one because of the complex United States immigration and naturalization laws.

Instead of simply bemoaning this situation, Saund helped start an organization called the India Association of America to press for legislation that would give his countrymen citizenship. Through a bill which the House and Senate passed and which President Truman signed in 1946, the objective was achieved. Saund immediately applied for citizenship and, after delays because of bureaucratic red tape, received his final papers in 1949.

No sooner had Saund been granted citizenship than he was named to the central committee of the Democratic party in Imperial County. In 1952 he was elected justice of the judicial district court in his own town of Westmoreland.

The small town of Westmoreland had for years been wide open for prostitution as masses of agricultural day laborers swarmed into the area at peak crop periods. Saund began handing out tough sentences against prostitutes and bawdyhouse operators, and Westmoreland was cleaned up.

Meanwhile Saund's agricultural ventures had brought him enough money to set up a successful fertilizer business. With one son and one daughter in college and another daughter married, he now had more time to devote to politics. After advancing to the chairmanship of the Imperial County Democratic Central Com-

*On pilgrimage to his birthplace, Chhajalwadi, in 1957, flower-swathed Saund stands with his wife, his Indian sister Ratan Kuar, and his daughter.*

*Some of the 4,000 who turned out to greet him wait with marigold garlands. They chanted, "Americans and Hindus are brothers."*

*During 1957 visit, Saund chats with Indian lawmaker, Ananthasayanam Ayyanger, Speaker of the Lower House.*

*Saund confers with United States lawmaker, Speaker of the House of Representatives Sam Rayburn, 1958.*

mittee, in 1956 he was ready to make his big jump into national politics: a bid for the United States House of Representatives.

United States congressional elections are held every two years, and in California each party chooses its nominees in a primary election in the early summer. The Democrat and the Republican who receive the most votes in the primaries become their parties' candidates in the November general election. This meant that Saund had to campaign in the primary almost as hard as he did in the subsequent election. After beating his Democratic party national opponents in the primary, he found himself squared off against the victor in an equally hard-fought Republican primary, Jacqueline Cochran.

He could scarcely have faced a more famous or formidable opponent than this handsome, forty-seven-year-old woman whose background was as remarkable as Saund's own. From a childhood as an orphan in a poverty-stricken southern town she had risen, through remarkable aviation exploits, to a vital wartime position as head of the WASPS, a group of women fliers who ferried planes from manufacturers to the nation's airfields. Moreover, she was head of a large cosmetics manufacturing firm and the wife of Floyd Odlum, one of the nation's most important financiers.

If Saund lacked such fame, wealth, and prestige, he was an equal match in energy for the indefatigable "Jackie" Cochran. While she zoomed around the Twenty-ninth Congressional District in her Lockheed Lodestar, Saund whipped across the desert in his 1956 Buick.

As in many United States congressional races, party issues were not nearly so important as personalities. In his campaign Saund generally stressed the issues that were closest to the valley's farmers and small businessmen, particularly federal aid to agriculture. Although Mrs. Odlum professed concern for the increasing centralization of the federal government, she too emphasized the valley's own problems and strongly backed President Eisenhower's farm program.

Not unexpectedly, racial and religious issues were injected during the campaign. Some supporters of Mrs. Odlum were heard to refer to Judge Saund as "that Hindu," and there was some innuendo that Hinduism was probably not much better than Communism. Some Saund supporters retaliated in kind with reference to Mrs. Odlum's being a Roman Catholic. But neither of the principals in the campaign considered such tactics worthy of notice, and apparently most voters did not either.

As against Miss Cochran's fame and glamor, Saund's main advantage was the fact that many in the Twenty-ninth District seemed to feel that he was closer to the voters than she was. For despite his foreign birth, Asian religion, and darker skin, many voters identified him first as an Imperial County farmer who had shared the good times and the bad and who had participated actively for years in the town affairs of Westmoreland.

Yet as Election Day neared, few people thought Saund had much of a chance. It was a presidential as well as congressional election year, and President Eisenhower was at the peak of his popularity. Every Republican candidate stood to share a bit of the President's luster. Yet when the votes of California's Twenty-ninth District had been counted, things did not turn out that way. Eisenhower had carried the Twenty-ninth overwhelmingly against Adlai Stevenson, but Dalip Singh Saund had defeated Jacqueline Cochran. Many voters had crossed party lines to vote for Saund. It was a tremendous personal victory.

In his post-election assessment Saund decided that the greatest thing in his favor had been the simple fact that he was of Indian extraction. "I think there were many, many people who liked this opportunity of demonstrating that they believed in democracy and fair play."

Although he has since been re-elected, Saund does not take his office for granted. He regularly interrupts his congressional chores to shuttle back and forth to California. Between meetings with constituents, Saund spends much time quietly at home with his family, some members of which have settled elsewhere around the United States but often return for family reunions. Saund still reads Indian literature and tries to keep up with news from his homeland. But mainly he is concerned with the future of his district, his state, and his new country. For, as he told his relatives and friends in Chhajalwadi during his last visit, "I have become part of American life."

*Saund family includes (behind Saund) Mrs. Saund, daughters Ellie and Julie; (rear) Dalip Jr., his wife Dorothy, and Julie's husband, Dr. Fred Fisher.*

# Gian Carlo Menotti

*Gian
Carlo
Menotti*

*Most Europeans go to America to seek their fortune. I for one went there to look for artistic guidance. To many of my colleagues in Europe, such a pilgrimage might sound almost heretical—but in my new home, I found an artistic nourishment which proved vital to the development of my craft. My comic operas could not have come to life, if not ignited by the spark of the American sense of humor—nor would my sense of compassion have so quickly extended itself out of the bounds of nationalism, had I not traveled so far.*

*Many are the important things I learned from America—how to face life with the joyous spontaneity of innocence, rather than the wariness of experience; how to accept criticism with grace, and how to smile at oneself; how to love the poor without envying the rich (for to love friends in distress comes much more easily to Italians than to love successful neighbors). What I found most astonishing in America is that almost any kind of person can find himself at home there—from the eccentric businessman to the shyest of artists.*

*Although unfortunately in most American communities, art is still considered an almost feminine luxury rather than a social necessity (hence the reason why so many American artists prefer living abroad), nowhere else in the world is an artistic experience more genuinely "desired."*

*The American people have often been judged superficial or materialistic as a whole by those visitors who are themselves unobservant and calculating. But those who come to America without arrogance and with a curious mind are sure to find deep friendship and boundless generosity.*

*by* T O M  P R I D E A U X

# Renaissance Man of American Music

WHEN the world thinks of American music, it usually thinks of United States jazz. Only in very recent years has there been an awareness that the United States has also developed a vast new interest in the more serious and traditional forms of music, and indeed that musical America is now training an impressive array of its own artists and composers. Among the latter none has attracted more acclaim in the United States and the rest of the world than an Italian-born writer of operas, ballets, and other works named Gian Carlo Menotti.

Menotti's long list of musical triumphs began when at the age of twenty-seven he won the honor, unprecedented for one so young, of seeing his first opera, *Amelia Goes to the Ball,* performed at New York's Metropolitan Opera House. Two of his subsequent works, *The Medium* and *The Consul,* have

93

achieved the near-impossible by winning both applause from serious music critics in the United States and abroad and commercial theater success too. A vast American public has awarded another Menotti opera, *Amahl and the Night Visitors,* the status of a television classic. Already firmly established as a foremost United States composer of serious music, Menotti achieved more fame abroad with the opening of his ambitious festival of music and the arts at Spoleto, Italy, and the première of his latest opera at the Brussels World's Fair.

Gian Carlo Menotti is a far cry from the common image of the United States immigrant from Italy, impoverished, bewildered, often forced into menial labor. Menotti was born wealthy, in a pink villa on Lake Lugano. His musical precocity was applauded and encouraged by his well-to-do parents almost from his infancy. When his mother took him to America in 1928 she carried a recommendation of her son's musical abilities from Arturo Toscanini.

In his rise to fame Menotti has faced only trivial hardships. His first United States piano teacher, at Philadelphia's Curtis Institute, summed up Menotti's good fortune. "He was like a sunshine," recalls Madame Vera Resnikoff. "Things seemed to go well with Gian Carlo just about all the time."

Yet, for all of his early advantages, Menotti in fact found the United States a land of opportunity just as truly as did many of the other five million Italians who have immigrated there in the past century. He was to become the most successful American composer of serious music because he had arrived in the country when it was uniquely ready for his unique talents.

Why were America and Menotti so receptive to each other? For one thing, the very lack of a strong musical tradition worked to Menotti's advantage. In Italy he would have been held up for comparison with the nation's great musical heroes: Verdi, Puccini, Rossini. In America, to a far greater extent, he could be judged simply as Menotti. Although most Americans had an avowed disinterest in grand opera, they were traditionally open-minded and curious about anything new. Like any lover courting a girl, Menotti found it was easier to overcome indifference than to supplant already-loved idols.

In any case, that indifference was fast being dispelled. Among the factors dispelling it was the phonograph, which, contrary to some gloomy expectations, did not foster a nation of passive listeners but instead developed greater audiences for "live" music and stimulated more and more people to create music of their own. Whereas opera used to be centered in New York, with two or three second-rate companies touring the country, today there are some 703 established opera groups scattered across the land, a large majority composed of impassioned amateurs. There are also 259 civic symphony orchestras —and an estimated twenty-eight million people who play at least one instrument.

Menotti has surely profited from being in America during its

*Student Menotti (left), shortly after his arrival in the United States, stands before the Curtis Institute with his friend Samuel Barber and a classmate.*

ABOVE: *Baby Gian Carlo* (far left) *lines up with older brothers and sisters on grounds of the family home at Cadegliano, Italy. There were five younger Menotti children.* BELOW: *Pink villa overlooking Lake Lugano was Menotti's childhood home. Here the Menotti children acted out plays in the garden and had their early musical education.*

years of musical awakening. In turn, he himself has hastened the awakening with music that is tuneful and original, operatic plots that are simply constructed and emotionally charged, and, above all, works that are theatrically and musically playable. The bridge between his creative genius and a receptive audience has been his own practicality.

This cheerful and mild-mannered young man, who adapted himself so well to the needs and temper of his adopted country, was the son of an Italian businessman. Alfonso Menotti made a small fortune in the South American import-export trade and then chose to settle down in the little town of Cadegliano and enjoy a quiet country life with his wife and eleven children. Gian Carlo's mother—an artistic woman who took up painting at sixty and the guitar at sixty-two—organized her offspring into drawing-room concerts. Everybody played or sang. She lavished special attention on Gian Carlo because he seemed to be the most talented.

By six he had decided to become a composer. He recalls setting "the most erotic little verses of D'Annunzio to angelic little tunes." By nine he was the impresario of his own marionette show with a company of fifty puppets, including dragons, princesses, wizards, and a devil who jiggled up and down in an evil-smelling cloud of smoke which Gian Carlo created backstage by burning sulphur.

When the family moved to Milan, Gian Carlo studied music at the Verdi Conservatory. He was habitually ensconced in his family's box at La Scala, where Toscanini was a resident conductor, and habitually invited to play the piano in elegant salons. Spoiled by friends and bored by routine school work, the prodigy was becoming something of a problem child.

After Signor Menotti's death in 1924, Signora Menotti took her son to South America and later to the United States. There, on the advice of musical friends, she installed him at Curtis Institute. His teachers warned Gian Carlo that he had to work hard, and he did.

Gian Carlo spoke Italian and French with his teachers, but his ignorance of English isolated him from his classmates. Shortly, how-

*Gian Carlo at ten served as a page at the wedding of his older sister Amalita.*

ever, he met another composition student, Samuel Barber, who spoke French. Sam invited Gian Carlo to his family's home for a traditional American celebration, Thanksgiving. The Barbers called their young guest Johnny and welcomed him so warmly over his first turkey dinner that Gian Carlo felt he had found a haven in America and a close friend in Sam. Their friendship—and musical association—continues to this day.

Thoroughly acclimated, Menotti continued to impress his other teachers at Curtis as he had Madame Resnikoff. After his graduation with honors in 1933 he was asked to join the school's faculty. Between teaching chores he went seriously to work on his first opera, *Amelia Goes to the Ball*. Not long after its première at Curtis there were inquiries from the Metropolitan in New York, and Menotti enjoyed his first triumph. Word soon got back to Italy and he received from the Italian Ambassador an offer, which he declined, of honorary membership in the Fascist party.

*Amelia* was followed by *The Old Maid and the Thief*, a radio opera commissioned by the National Broadcasting Company; it was another instant success. This was followed by *The Island God*,

Menotti's second work produced by the Metropolitan Opera; it was an instant flop. Menotti profited by his failure. For *The Island God* he had written some beautiful music, but the opera itself was a static, philosophical discourse on morality, which taught the composer to stick closer to richly dramatic situations not too far removed from the dragons, wizards, and sulphur smoke of his childhood.

He applied the lesson superbly well to *The Medium,* his two-act chamber opera that made theater history in 1947 by playing 212 consecutive performances—more than any other opera had ever been given in the United States. *The Medium* was performed together with a short Menotti curtain raiser called *The Telephone,* which led to frequent misapprehension along Broadway that the production was a full-length opera with the baffling title of *The Medium and The Telephone.*

*The Medium* is a chilling tale, half grand opera and half Grand Guignol, about a fraudulent spiritualist who cheats her followers by calling up fake ghosts and then goes insane with fear and kills her assistant after she imagines that she has actually been touched by an icy hand from beyond the grave.

"Despite its eerie setting and gruesome conclusions," says Menotti, *"The Medium* is actually a play of ideas. It describes the tragedy of a woman caught between two worlds, a world of reality which she cannot wholly comprehend, and a supernatural world in which she cannot believe." The theme of *The Medium* had occurred to Menotti as he watched the ardent believers at a private séance.

To possibly a greater extent, Menotti's next production, *The Consul,* was also a play of ideas and certainly a play of two worlds. Its Kafka-like heroine, Magda Sorel, struggles to escape from an unnamed European police state—a brutal world of idiotic bureaucracy—and join her husband who has fled to a more enlightened world. For most of the opera Magda sits in the consul's anteroom, waiting for her visa, filling out endless, meaningless questionnaires. Writing essentially of man's inhumanity to man, Menotti reached his highest eloquence in Magda's second-act aria:

*What is your name? Magda Sorel.*
*Age? Thirty-three.*
*What does that matter. . . ?*
*What is your name?*
*What is your name?*
*What is your name?*
*This is my answer: my name is woman. Age: still young.*
*Color of hair: gray. Color of eyes: the color of tears.*
*Occupation: waiting, waiting, waiting.*

And Magda ends her hopeless waiting with her head in a gas oven.

When favorable reviews began to pour in after *The Consul's* opening, Menotti delivered a warning to himself and his proud associates not to be carried away by their success. He later explained, "Artists must be very stubborn. What defeats the artist in America today is his willingness to compromise in order to achieve success."

*The Consul* went on to success not only on Broadway but in many parts of Europe where its theme of freedom-hungry people struggling to escape their bondage struck home. Among the works of art emerging from World War II, *The Consul* is one of the most moving and will probably be one of the longest remembered.

Despite his humility, Menotti was not quite prepared for what happened a year later in Milan. None of his earlier works had been well received in Italy, but optimistically he accepted an invitation to stage *The Consul* at La Scala. To celebrate the opening he bought new full-dress evening clothes, his first since he was thirteen years old. A dozen members of his family, who had never been much impressed by the reports of his success, were coming to observe Gian Carlo's gala night.

Menotti plunged into his job of directing rehearsals, which went on daily for almost two months. Two singers were imported from the American cast; the rest were from Italy. It was hard enough to enlarge *The Consul*—an intimate opera on Broadway—to fill the vast La Scala stage. It was harder to challenge centuries of operatic tradition. The singers were co-operative but dumfounded when

Menotti asked them to act intensely on stage, even when they were not actually singing.

Before opening night there were darker mutterings in the musical circles of Milan. Many Italians were resentful that Menotti had won his fame in the United States. The Communists resented the libretto, which they already knew to be scornfully antitotalitarian. And then came a final omen of disaster. The white doves that the magician was supposed to release in the second act had been delivered to the singer's apartment: the cook had baked them for dinner.

Just before the overture, a leading critic of Milan's *Il Tempo* stalked into a box with seven friends, all equipped with whistles. They were upholding tradition at La Scala, where even Verdi and Puccini had faced boos and critical brickbats, and every red-blooded Italian still considers opera important enough to fight over. The curtain was barely up on *The Consul* when the whistles began to toot. While the singers strained their lungs and Menotti paled in the wings, the audience began its obbligato of boos and bravos.

Shrieked one woman, "Down with Americans! Long live Italy! This is a dirty mess!"

One of La Scala's conductors, defending Menotti, stood up in the audience and roared, *"Cretini! Stupidi! Ignoranti!"*

The performance continued. So did the uproar. To the bitter end the hullabaloo persisted. And after composer and cast had taken eleven curtain calls to the applause of the many in the audience who liked the opera, the tumult spilled into the streets; amid the flying fists two music lovers were arrested. Next morning most of the critics continued their attack in the newspapers, calling the opera "old-fashioned" and "impotent." The controversy went on through *The Consul's* subsequent four performances in Milan. Everywhere else in Europe *The Consul* opened noisily but without violence. London cheered; Paris threw hats; and Basel, Switzerland, surpassed everybody by giving forty-five curtain calls.

Menotti's talents were still being appreciated in the United States, and not in the theaters alone. United States television, riding the wave of opera's new popularity, now beckoned him. In 1950 the National Broadcasting Company commissioned Menotti to write a Christmas television opera. They gave him nearly two years to meet the deadline. But Menotti, who is the soul of dependability at the eleventh hour, often causes terrible consternation at the tenth. By September, only three months before the deadline, he had not written a note. In despair his sponsors thought they might have to abandon the project. Then one day while wandering through New York's Metropolitan Museum, Menotti saw *The Adoration of the Magi* by Hieronymus Bosch. The picture of the Three Kings offering their gifts to the Christ Child reminded him of Italy, where children believe their gifts are brought not by Santa Claus but by the Three Kings. Suddenly he was aglow with memories of his own childhood.

As a small child Gian Carlo had been crippled in one leg. A devout nurse had taken him to a shrine of the Madonna, and soon afterward he had been cured. Menotti today believes his cure may have been a miracle, though he confesses to skepticism and has long since left the Roman Catholic Church. He continues to say, however, "I have faith in faith." Now he concocted a charming, sentimental little opera about a crippled shepherd boy, Amahl, who is visited by the Kings and miraculously cured of his lameness.

In his final rush to complete *Amahl,* Menotti worked all day, and every night a messenger rushed a few more pages of Amahl's aria to the twelve-year-old boy soprano who had to start rehearsing the role bit by bit. To finish his orchestrations, Menotti called in a group of his students and dictated separate parts to each of them, saying, "This is for flute. This is for oboe," and so on. As it turned out, *Amahl* is a small masterpiece of childlike innocence and reverence, and of all Menotti's works, it is best known and most loved in America.

In 1954 came Menotti's most ambitious work, *The Saint of Bleecker Street.* The opera is set in the Italian immigrant section of New York, which Menotti had never seen until he made two visits there to watch a religious parade and absorb local color for his drama. But though he was a stranger to the poor Italian immigrant's world, he was Italian enough to write feelingly and authentically about them because they were his own people. His young heroine is a humble and sickly "saint" who one Good Friday has a vision of the Cross and shows Christ's stigmata. Her devoted brother tries to save her from what he holds to be religious fanaticism. After a profusion of liturgical choruses, soaring arias, lyrical Tuscan folk songs, a jukebox dance number, and a bitter lament sung in the subway, the saint and her brother meet separate deaths. Their conflict Menotti deliberately leaves unresolved.

*The Saint of Bleecker Street,* thought by many Americans to be his best opera, won Menotti two coveted honors: the New York Drama Critics' Circle Award and the Pulitzer Prize for 1955. The composer was convinced it would be his most popular work in Italy and felt that as a grand-scale opera it would meet the demands of La Scala. When it was produced there in 1956 there was none of the previous commotion, but none of the critical adulation of the United States, either.

Demonstrating that he could compose ballet as successfully as opera, Menotti completed in 1957 *The Unicorn, the Gorgon and the Manticore.* In twelve madrigals sung by a choral group, and six orchestral interludes, the ballet describes the secret heart of a poet, evoking the mythological creatures of Menotti's fancy, and telling how lovingly they have served him through his whole life. The ballet, which is one of Menotti's finest works, was first performed in Washington's Library of Congress and went on to a successful run in New York.

On the ballet or operatic stage Menotti is, above all, a master showman. His music is both original and eclectic. To suit his purpose, he may fall into the musical styles of Puccini, Moussorgsky, Debussy, or almost any other composer, but manages in the end to achieve his own feeling and flavor. He writes simple plots, highly charged with emotion. Audiences, in fact, are sometimes so absorbed by his stories that they forget they are listening to music. For Menotti this is a great compliment; he believes his music should serve to heighten, never intrude upon, the total dramatic effect. To this end he writes all of his own librettos in impressively clear and singable English, despite, or perhaps because of, the fact that it was not his native tongue. He always directs the first performances of all his operas to make sure they are in every way stageworthy.

Most of Menotti's works have been composed at a country house set in seventy acres of hilly woodland near Mt. Kisco, New York, which he shares with his old friend Sam Barber, who has also become one of America's leading composers. Each musician has his own studio in a separate wing of the house so their busy pianos cannot clash. In the spring of 1958 Barber's first opera, *Vanessa,* was presented successfully for the first time at the Metropolitan Opera, and it had its European première on August 16, 1958, at the Salzburg Music Festival. Menotti wrote the libretto for *Vanessa*—the only time he has ever written words for another composer's music.

With a motherly cook to watch over the establishment, Menotti likes to gather friends for social weekends. He loves long philosophical arguments and gossip. In his desk he keeps a collection of newspaper clippings about weird events, freaks of nature, and dramatic crimes. Not long ago his friends were surprised, but not too surprised, to hear him announce that he wanted to rid himself of all earthly possessions and live in a cave. He even went so far as to compile a list of what he planned to take with him: "Two suits, three shirts, two pairs of shoes, and three pairs of socks."

Although he has done most of his work and found his most responsive audiences in the United States, Menotti retains his deep affection for Italy—which is probably why he has never gotten around to taking out United States citizenship. Most summers since World War II he has been off for Italy, and for several years he dreamed of founding there an American-Italian "Festival of Two Worlds," dedicated to music, drama, ballet, and fine arts. During the summer of 1956, after scouting all over Italy, Menotti picked a setting for his dream—the hill town of Spoleto eighty miles north of Rome—and set out to raise funds for the twenty-four-day festival, which opened on June 5, 1958.

Menotti brought into play the legendary powers of persuasion which enabled him in America to obtain backing for his artistic ventures—from broadcasting companies, philanthropic organizations, and private individuals—on a scale unequaled since the great days of royal patronage in Europe. After Menotti's charm had cracked such hard eleemosynary nuts as the United States State Department, the Italian government, and the Ford Foundation, a long list of private Italian and United States donors fell into line behind the Spoleto project.

Menotti drummed up talent on an even more fabulous scale. He cajoled three noted American artists, Alexander Calder, Ben Shahn, and Saul Steinberg, to design costumes and scenery for a group of new American ballets—without pay. Picasso has contributed

*Preparing for Menotti's "Festival of Two Worlds" in Spoleto, Italy, dancers practice in town square as children watch.*

the set for one production. The performers in the festival agreed to work merely for their expenses.

To help prepare Spoleto, Menotti arrived on the scene two months ahead of the June 1958 opening and concerned himself with everything under the sun. He readied two theaters and supervised the modernization of an old inn which he had bought and playfully rechristened "Albergo del Matto" (Inn of the Madman) after hearing the townspeople's amused references to his frantic activities. He opened festival offices, attended rehearsals, checked tourist bus schedules, and listened to the excited advice of plasterers, plumbers, contractors, and all their cousins. Between times he worked on his new opera for the Brussels Fair, *Maria Golevin,* which, of course, was far from finished.

Though he currently seems to be conducting himself like a Renaissance art patron, Menotti is not given to self-glorification. He refused to let any of his own music be performed at Spoleto and refused to say how much of his own money he gave to the festival. His friends say he tossed in every dollar he had. Spoleto was an artistic and popular success, but it did indeed lose money. It thus enabled Menotti to unite two sides of his complex nature—to play both the prince and the pauper at the same time.

With all of his own intellectual conflicts and his dual allegiance to America and Italy, Menotti was surely the ideal impresario for a Festival of Two Worlds. Both worlds have profited richly from his presence. The happiest circumstance of all is that, although Menotti lives most of the time in America, he has retained his warm, essentially Italian genius. Speaking of his music, and speaking like a true Italian, he says, "I want to move the human heart, and that's all I want."

*At Spoleto, Menotti sits on the slopes of Monte Luco, overlooking the ancient Roman town where he held his famous international festival.*

*David Dubinsky*

## David Dubinsky

*The American labor movement recognizes that the common struggle against the totalitarian menace demands that all democratic free trade unions—Socialist, Catholic, Protestant, and the so-called pure and simple type—must unite their ranks on an international scale. . . . Judging by the fantastic notions that some people abroad hold about our country, a darker and more forbidding Atlantic now hides America from the rest of the world than in the days of . . . Columbus. By full participation in the international free trade union movement, American unionism can make a major contribution toward rediscovery of America—the real America—by the people of the Old World.*

*by* SERRELL HILLMAN

# *Pacemaker for Labor*

PARIS is still indisputably the world center of women's fashion design, and today as for centuries past no man can be called impeccably dressed unless he is tailored by London's elegant Savile Row. But the place where styles and trends are set most swiftly for the most men and women is a noisy, jam-packed area on the west side of Manhattan Island.

Through the genius of this New York garment center, within a short while after a society leader introduces an $800 Paris original, a United States debutante will be seen in a $150 adaptation of it, a suburban matron will buy it for a cocktail party at $69.50, and a United States stenographer will go to a bridal shower in a modified version costing $14.95. Each year the garment industry, New York City's biggest business, supplies American women with six billion dollars' worth of just about everything that goes into their closets and bureau drawers. Each year 380,000 workers, 65 per cent of them women, turn out 16,000,000 women's coats, 9,000,000 women's suits, 105,000,000 dresses, 8,000,000 men's suits and coats in a jumble of small, mussy workrooms crammed into grimy loft buildings and nondescript factory structures.

In the narrow streets of the garment district pedestrians are in constant danger of being clipped by the countless handcarts piled high with coats or dresses and trundled at an alarming rate from one building to another. Each day around noon in the area the sharp whir of sewing machines slows down, and workers and bosses pour onto the grimy sidewalks, shout in Yiddish, Italian, Spanish, and English above the harsh brays of automobile horns. Upstairs at their tables some garment workers munch sandwiches from paper bags and enjoy their one relaxation in the day. After an hour the work-rooms shake again to a familiar clatter as machines hum and whir and snap, stop and start.

The women's clothing capital of the world is dominated not by any manufacturer or group of manufacturers, but by a labor leader who, at the age of eighteen, came to the United States in 1911 from Lodz, Poland, with twenty dollars in his pockets. To the 445,000 members of his International Ladies' Garment Workers' Union, crop-haired, pudgy David Dubinsky is more than boss; he is prophet, father, and demigod. To the managements of most of the 12,500 United States and Canadian firms who have contracts with the I.L.G., Dubinsky is a symbol of honest, imaginative unionism.

The American success story of David Dubinsky is virtually synonymous with the success story of the International Ladies' Garment Workers' Union. And the story of the I.L.G., as most unionists call it, keynotes the success story of labor in the United States. The I.L.G. has pioneered in winning health and welfare benefits, in building medical centers and vacation resorts for its members. No union has given so generously for foreign relief and rehabilitation or tried harder to cement ties between United States and overseas unions.

In a period which has seen the whole United States labor movement under fire for the scandalously corrupt practices revealed within some other unions, Dubinsky stands out as labor's most inveterate fighter against union corruption. Inside and outside his union he has also fought Communism relentlessly. As one who fled Czarist oppression, he once wrote of "the bitter advantage that is mine in having seen the dark side of the moon."

David Dubinsky was born David Dobnievski, February 22, 1892, at Brest-Litovsk, then part of Russian Poland, the eighth of nine children. When David was seven, his father moved to the grimy industrial city of Lodz and set up a small bakery. The bakery consisted of a single room, the middle of which was dwarfed by a huge oven. Behind it was the family's one bedroom, where David's father, stepmother, and older brother, Chaim, all slept. In the winter David slept in the shabby kitchen; in summer his bed was a delivery wagon in the back yard near the outhouse.

At the age of fourteen David had absorbed so much knowledge of baking that his father put him to work as a master baker. Like other bakers David worked twelve to fifteen hours a day, six days a week. Yet he found time for his earliest union activity. At fifteen he was elected secretary of his bakers' local despite his age.

Soon the brash young unionist had devised a share-the-work plan to limit unemployment by preventing each baker from working one given night a week. In January 1908 the czarist police, convinced that the bakers' union represented rebellion against the Czar, seized Dubinsky and other local leaders at a secret meeting.

Without the formality of charges or a trial Dubinsky was sentenced to an indefinite term of exile in Siberia. The machinery of injustice moved so slowly that it took him sixteen months to get there. During stopovers at the Paviak prison at Warsaw and the Butyrki prison at Moscow, he read Marx and Engels and became excited by Marxian socialism. With fellow prisoners, he argued politics late into the night while innumerable wriggling bedbugs in the dirty straw mattresses made sleep impossible.

*Dubinsky in Poland, aged sixteen, when he was employed in his father's bakery.*

Finally Dubinsky was put on a train for western Siberia. "We rode to the border," says Dubinsky, "and were ordered out of the train. In Siberia you didn't ride; you walked from village to village."

After ten days on the road Dubinsky determined to escape to the town of Chelyabinsk, where he knew that political exiles enjoyed comparative freedom. He escaped simply by walking away from the building where the group had stopped for the night. Making his way to Chelyabinsk, he spent six months working in a bakery, unmolested by police. "Once you were in Siberia," he explains, "they didn't care what you did." Finally he decided to return to Lodz despite the police ban against him. His father wired him twenty-five rubles in care of a rabbi friend.

In no great hurry to reach home, Dubinsky paused several weeks at Bialystok, Poland, where he again plied his baker's trade. He stopped at several other cities, befriended in each by political revolutionaries, before he returned to Lodz. There he went back to work as a baker under an assumed name and changed his sleeping place every night to avoid arrest.

Finally David's brothers Jacob and Hyman, who had migrated to the United States several years earlier, stepped in to end an impossible situation. Both had thrived as bakers in New York, and Hyman was doing well enough to send David a boat ticket. Jacob sent a ticket to their brother Chaim. The two boys were smuggled across the border and at Antwerp boarded the *Lapland,* which carried freight and a live cargo of seven hundred steerage passengers, including Polish and Romanian Jews and Hungarians bound for the steel mills and coal mines of Pennsylvania.

After a rough eleven-day crossing the *Lapland* reached New York on the cold, misty afternoon of Sunday, January 1, 1911. When Dubinsky greeted his Americanized brothers at the dock, he carried one tattered suitcase full of dirty underclothes. "I had one suit which I was wearing on me," he says, "and the pants were torn in back."

For several months David and Chaim lived with Jacob in lower Manhattan, then found lodgings of their own. Dubinsky quickly decided to abandon baking. "I didn't like the hours," he says, "and I hated the heat." Dubinsky looked enviously at the aristocracy of the needle trades, the cutters. But three years' experience were required for membership in the International Garment Workers' Cutters' Local 10. "Easy it wasn't," says Dubinsky. "A little forgery was needed."

His sister-in-law wrote out an affidavit saying he had worked for three years in a dry-cleaning store where some cutting was done. A foreman who, like Dubinsky, had grown up in Lodz consented to hire him in return for a fifty-dollar tip. Within a year Dubinsky had become a skilled cutter in fact as well as in title. "I was a close marker," he says, meaning that he was able to cut fabric to a pattern without wasting the cloth.

Within six months of his arrival Dubinsky had joined the American Socialist party. Although the party's principles were founded in Marxist philosophy, its leader, Eugene Debs, was a gentle and somewhat vague theorist who believed in socialism through orderly evolution. In 1912 the party's strength reached its highest point when Debs got 900,672 votes for President of the United States. (The election was won by Woodrow Wilson with 6,000,000 votes.)

Dubinsky enthusiastically carried soapboxes from one Socialist rally to another and became a fiery and effective speaker in English as well as Yiddish. Today he speaks English with tumbling, headlong fluency but retains an accent about which he is extremely sensitive.

The Socialists' influence waned badly after 1913, when the liberal Democratic administration of President Wilson enacted some of the legislation for which the Socialists had fought. When World War I came, the Socialists were badly split. Debs went to jail for opposing the war; many other Socialist leaders also took pacifist stands. Dubinsky, however, supported the war stoutly and made a number of speeches urging unionists to buy Liberty bonds. The Socialists never recaptured a position of importance. By 1928 Dubinsky had ceased to be a regular supporter.

The I.L.G., in whose activities Dubinsky began taking a bigger part as his enthusiasm for socialism waned, had been formed in 1900, more than a decade before he had arrived in the United States. The founders had been eleven men with only thirty dollars between them. At that time almost all of the garment industry workers were new immigrants. Fleeing oppression and poverty in Europe, they flooded New York, settling in the lower East Side. Homesick, handicapped by language difficulties, they seemed the perfect answer to a new industry's demand for cheap labor. Workers were herded into dirty, airless rooms, forced to rent the sewing machines they used, to pay for electric power, for needles and thread, and even for the hooks on which they hung their hats. They worked seventy hours a week for a five-dollar salary.

Until 1910 the I.L.G. made little progress. Then three dramatic events turned the tide. Two were victories, the other was a tragedy. The I.L.G. won two great New York City strikes involving shirtwaist and cloak makers. Out of the cloak strike came a Protocol of Peace, which set a pattern of labor stability far in advance of the rest of United States unionism by establishing boards of arbitration and labor-management committees to inspect sanitary conditions and set piece rates.

The tragedy was the Triangle Waist Company fire, which took 146 lives on March 25, 1911. The victims, most of them girl workers, had little chance to escape. The single fire escape of their ten-story building in the heart of the garment district was inadequate and an exit leading to the stairway was bolted. The girls, their hair and clothing ablaze, hurled themselves to the street, falling with such force that many tore holes in the nets spread by firemen. New York City was appalled by the disaster and mortified by its own failure

*Shortly after his arrival in the United States, Dubinsky worked as a cutter in New York's garment industry.*

to provide safe factories for its workers. One result was that even anti-union elements quickly accepted the I.L.G.'s right to speak for garment labor.

By 1930 Dubinsky had become one of the major powers in the I.L.G., largely as a result of the leadership he gave in a disastrous strike. In their vigorous infiltration of United States labor during the 1920s the Communists had been attracted to the I.L.G., and by 1926 they controlled all of the union except Dubinsky's own Cutters' Local 10 and two Italian-language locals. If the Communists had managed to capture Local 10, they would have been able to take over the whole union, since if the cutters stop work, everything stops. Under Dubinsky's determined leadership Local 10 remained solidly anti-Communist. But in the 1926 strike Local 10 went out with the rest of the union. Although unable to keep the men at work, Dubinsky was successful in keeping the Communists from control of the International executive board and so enraged them by his hostility that he was forced to carry a gun for protection.

After eight weeks it was apparent that the strike was a failure. Dubinsky and other anti-Communists urged a settlement. The Communists insisted on keeping the workers out for another nineteen weeks, and the union was finally forced to settle for fewer benefits than it could have gained by peaceful negotiation. The strike cost the I.L.G. three and a half million dollars, but it demolished Communist prestige and made Dubinsky's reputation.

The union's troubles were far from over. Barely had it recovered from the strike and the Communist infiltration than the great depression struck. By now Dubinsky was secretary-treasurer of the International. Untroubled by the fact that the union treasury contained nothing but IOUs, he met his first depression crisis resourcefully. When workers in a branch of the New York dress industry struck, the employers counted on an early surrender by the impoverished strikers. Dubinsky wrote out a check for $50,000 to the union strike committee. At the next bargaining session between strikers and employers the strike committee chairman "accidentally" dropped the check from his pocket and made sure that the employers saw it. The management negotiators, thinking they were up against a much more formidable opponent than they had expected, hastily settled.

Yet not all Dubinsky's cunning strategy could disguise the fact that the union was in pitiful shape. By 1932, as more and more garment workers lost their jobs, membership had gone down from a 1919 peak of 129,000 to a mere 28,000. Union officers no longer received salaries; they got $15 or $20 "on account." Manufacturers took full advantage of the union's weakness, and sweatshop conditions began to return to the industry. When Dubinsky was elected president of the I.L.G. in 1932, fellow unionists wryly congratulated him on becoming "chief undertaker."

That same year Franklin D. Roosevelt was elected President of the United States. He set out to give labor what he and his Democratic party regarded as a New Deal. Dubinsky was delighted with Roosevelt's promises. Counting on support from Washington, he set about organizing garment strikes throughout the United States.

In May 1933 the I.L.G. walked out in Philadelphia; in August it struck in New York. Backed by New Deal policies, the I.L.G. won immediate success. By January 1, 1934, the union had 198,000 members and money in the bank. Says Dubinsky, "At the 1934 union convention I was like God. Of course, it wasn't me, it was Roosevelt who was responsible. But I got the credit."

While Dubinsky's ambitions for the I.L.G. and the rest of labor were being fulfilled, he was having trouble with his fellow leaders of the American Federation of Labor. Dubinsky was among a number of leaders who tried to persuade the hidebound A.F.L. hierarchy that the concept of many craft unions was outdated and that industry-wide unions were bound to come throughout the United States. But Dubinsky and his cohorts tried in vain to keep the A.F.L. from splitting on the issues of industrial vs. craft unionism. When the split came Dubinsky at first kept his I.L.G. independent of both the A.F.L. and the new Congress of Industrial Or-

*Garment district of New York is a jammed area with narrow streets usually clogged by trucks and handcarts.*

ganizations. Eighteen months later he brought the I.L.G. back into the A.F.L.

To this day, although Dubinsky has received surprisingly little open criticism, there are those in the labor movement who accuse him of being a benevolent despot. Some dress manufacturers argue that he has built a gigantic machine which, in unscrupulous hands, could crush the industry, while some unionists accuse Dubinsky of being too intimate with the employers. All of this seems insignificant to Dubinsky alongside his feeling of what the I.L.G. means to United States labor and what labor means to David Dubinsky. With typical immodesty, he says, "I got no regrets. In fact, I can't think of any mistakes I've made, and that's bad. I don't know how it happened, but everything I've done turned out to be right."

Dubinsky is especially proud of his consistently international attitude toward foreign labor. In 1947 Dubinsky came out solidly for the Marshall Plan when some isolationist-minded A.F.L. leaders were reluctant and some Communist-dominated C.I.O. unions were frankly opposed. At the I.L.G. convention that year Dubinsky introduced a resolution backing the Marshall Plan and asking the A.F.L. to call an international conference of free trade unions.

In 1948 Dubinsky was a delegate at London where for the first time free trade unions got together on a world-wide basis. Out of that conference the International Confederation of Free Trade Unions was formed in 1949. Today the I.C.F.T.U. is recognized everywhere as the world voice of free labor, while the World Federation of Trade Unions, founded in 1945, speaks only for Communism.

Dubinsky goes overseas almost every year to attend conferences and compare notes with foreign labor leaders. He has made only one trip to Russia since his escape from the Czar's police fifty years ago. In 1931, with his wife, he went to visit her parents in Lithuania and took a brief junket to Russia. "When I was in Moscow," he recalls, "I saw no picture of Trotsky in the Museum of Social History. How can you doctor or ignore history like that?"

He met his wife soon after coming to the United States, at a co-operative restaurant which Dubinsky and nine friends formed for $10 apiece. Emma Goldberg was a handsome, vivacious sewing-machine operator who had recently migrated from Kowno, Lithuania. When Dubinsky first knew her she was already an ardent member of Local 62 (the undergarment workers) of I.L.G., and she has never lost her enthusiasm for the union.

Dubinsky—known to his friends as "D.D."—is still an alarming bundle of energy and a bewildering mixture of characteristics. He is vain, irascible, sentimental, and ruthless; captious but charming, overbearing but humble. He can be difficult but never dull. Says his only child, Jean: "He has an original mind. It isn't a repository of other people's clichés."

The Dubinskys live in a six-room $200-a-month apartment on the top floor of a twenty-story building ("Don't call it a penthouse; it sounds bad"). For years Dubinsky refused to take a salary higher than $15,000 a year. Today he makes $26,000—still considerably less than that paid to many union presidents ($50,000 each to the mine-workers' John L. Lewis, the steelworkers' David J. McDonald, and the operating engineers' Joseph Delaney). It is, however, a source of constant irritation to many of Dubinsky's staff employees that he refuses to pay them appropriate wages (organizers make $125 a week, about $50 below the average in other big unions). Dubinsky's defense: "If we took more we would not give a damn about the workers."

At one point the union grew tired of watching Dubinsky cadge rides and bought him an automobile. But, embarrassed by his new chauffeur-driven Chrysler, he took his first driving lessons and now often drives his own English Ford. But his favorite method of transportation is his English-made bicycle. He bikes almost every Sunday in Manhattan's Central Park with his granddaughter, Ryna.

Dubinsky still lives and thrives on a brutal schedule. He is up every morning at 7:30 to punish himself with an ice-cold shower. He works prodigious hours and is at his desk in the I.L.G.'s million-dollar building until late most evenings.

Possessed of a gigantic appetite, Dubinsky developed a fondness for gorging himself at Lindy's, a theatrical restaurant on Broadway, with mammoth portions of onion rolls, pastrami, spiced pickles, and marinated herring, washed down with enough Scotch whisky or rum to stun a longshoreman. Lately, however, his doctor has ordered him to be more abstemious and he periodically tortures himself with rigid sessions of dieting in which he loses up to twenty-five pounds in a month.

Dubinsky likes to keep the I.L.G. reins firmly in hand. Besides

*Favorite recreation for Dubinsky is cycling. With grand-daughter he pedals down New York's Seventh Avenue, the heart of the garment district.*

the office of president he still holds onto that of secretary-treasurer, despite the criticism of many of his union colleagues. His answer to such criticism is characteristic: "In some unions you got a big problem with fighting between the president and the secretary-treasurer. In our union there's excellent relations." Still a passionate organizer, he has been known to attend even to such minor details as arranging the seating at funerals of I.L.G. officials. At union conventions he busies himself moving chairs and helping waiters set up banquet tables.

David Dubinsky has done as much as any United States unionist to make labor a respected force on the United States scene. Under his leadership the I.L.G. has donated twenty-five million·dollars to foreign relief and rehabilitation—far more than any other union. In 1948 it lent the new state of Israel one mililon dollars and is building a two-million-dollar hospital in that country. It is investing in a big Puerto Rican housing project; it runs a trade school in Paris and helps support a boys' town in Italy.

The I.L.G. can well afford its philanthropy. It has a bulging treasury of $246,000,000, most of it, of course, earmarked for health, welfare, and retirement benefits. In its elaborate vacation resort, Unity House, a member can get all his meals, swimming, boating, tennis, and dancing every night for $45 a week. On New York City's lower East Side the union has put up a twelve-acre co-operative housing development which cost $20,000,000. The union treats 150,000 persons a year at its New York medical center and operates eighteen health centers and clinics elsewhere in the United States.

But Dubinsky's I.L.G. looks farther afield than its own activities. On the principle that the garment workers' lot is only as good as that of the garment industry itself, the union has even gone so far as to build a plant and lease it to a manufacturer, and also maintains its own staff of industrial engineers to help employers improve their efficiency. Its record of harmonious co-operation with management has been broken only once since 1933. This was in the spring of 1958, when the union walked out, demanding adjustment in certain wages and hours and the end of preferential treatment for some manufacturers. The strike was settled amicably in six days.

A major reason for the remarkable harmony that has usually existed between garment labor and management is the singular respect the employers have for Dubinsky. His honesty is beyond question. In 1940 he pushed through the first A.F.L. resolution attacking corruption inside the ranks of labor. In 1955 he again pioneered when he became the first union leader to call for government legislation to curb corruption in the handling of union welfare funds.

It is only because of the pioneering of such men as Dubinsky that United States labor has learned to clean its own house. Thus America has been afforded the dramatic spectacle of Dave Beck's racket-ridden, though wealthy and powerful, Teamsters Union being thrown out of the parent A.F.L.-C.I.O. by the A.F.L.-C.I.O. leaders themselves. Dubinsky, a leader in the cleanup movement, celebrated in typical style. "It's a great day for a guy who has spent so much of his life working for clean unions," he said as he gulped a Scotch and soda at a little Jewish restaurant right after the balloting had taken place. He shouted exuberantly, wriggled his feet, and twitched in his chair like a child at church. When a waiter, unnerved by these antics, carelessly brought him a beer, Dubinsky waved away the man's stammered apologies. "Never mind!" he bellowed. "I drink this too!"

Partly because of its huge powers and the few bosses who have abused those powers, United States labor has found itself at a critical turning point. If it goes ahead instead of backward, it will be because of leaders like David Dubinsky.

*Irving Berlin*

# Irving Berlin

*I came here as an immigrant from Russia in 1893 and whatever success I have had as a song writer I owe to this country. I have tried to express my feelings in "God Bless America," a song I wrote some years ago which is not alone a song, but an expression of my gratitude to the country that inspired it.*

*by* T O M  P R I D E A U X

# Mr. *"Words and Music"*

FOR the past fifty years Americans have had an in-
ordinate appetite for popular music. In contrast to
Europe, with its rich store of folk songs and regional
dance music, America has had to manufacture a great
many of its own songs for everyday singing. In recent
years the United States has discovered its own heritage
of native music—from the mountains of Kentucky and
Virginia, from the cowboys of the West and the Negroes of New Orleans. But Americans have been
mostly obliged, and temperamentally disposed, to sing
the newest up-to-the-minute songs composed by commercial tunesmiths. Popular music has helped unite
the United States. It has helped a highly diversified
people, separated by great distances and speaking in
many different accents, to feel they belong to the same
family.

America's need for popular music appears, almost mystically, to have evoked the presence of Irving Berlin, whose first song was published more than fifty years ago, and who has published more songs (750) than any other living United States composer. Whenever the occasion called for music, Irving Berlin, by a compulsion that has directed his entire life, rose to the occasion. Coming to the United States as a Russian Jewish immigrant at the age of four, Berlin appeared to set out to prove that the American legend is really true.

He proved that America can be a haven for the downtrodden (his family fled to the United States to escape religious persecution).

He proved that poverty is no obstacle to success (he has earned more money from his songs than any other composer in history).

He proved that humble origins are not a social barrier (he married a mutimillionairess of high social position).

This prototypal immigrant, whose original name was Israel Baline, was born in 1888 in the village of Temun in Siberian Russia. He remembers huddling all night with his family in a frosty field and seeing the nightmare glow of his town after it had been afire by Cossacks who swept down on the Jews of Temun. His father, Rabbi Moses Baline, packed up his wife and six of his children (a son and daughter remained in Russia) and headed for America. When the Balines finally arrived in New York, and his mother, Leah, stepped into their two-room flat, she whispered, with shining eyes, "Das Goldene Land."

The Golden Land was slow to open up its treasures for the Balines. Moses found poorly paid work as a cantor in synagogues, as a teacher of Hebrew in neighborhood homes, and as a *mashgi'ach* supervising observance of religious laws in kosher meat markets. The children helped by selling newspapers and doing bead work by the murky light of their basement window. When his father died, Israel was eight years old. But though he tried even harder to sell papers, he had a livelier interest in pitching pennies, hurling his crickety little body into street brawls, and diving into the East River at the foot of Cherry Street where he moved with his family to a new but scarcely more commodious home.

One afternoon he stopped at a dock to watch a freighter loading cargo for China. A bundle of unsold newspapers was clamped under his arm. Five pennies were squeezed in his hand. A crane got out of control and swung against Israel, batting him into the river. The passers-by laughed at the little urchin floundering in the oily water. Valor finally appeared in the form of another urchin, who jumped in and dragged the future composer ashore.

An ambulance rushed him to a hospital where a doctor pumped the water out of Israel's lungs. The doctor commented that Israel had swallowed almost all of the East River. He also noted that the waterlogged newsboy still had a death grip on his five pennies.

Those who study the primal sources of human behavior might interpret the river episode as a sure sign that Israel was bound to acquire, and hold on to, great wealth. But in the light of his case history, the episode appears to bear more directly on Berlin's anxiety about his work. Whatever the job at hand, whether it be earning a few pennies or creating a Broadway show, he has always felt a gnawing responsibility to deliver what is expected of him—come what may.

It was because Israel at the age of fourteen felt he was not delivering enough toward his family's upkeep that he ran away from home. He slept under tenement stairways, grabbed free lunches in saloons, and joined an old Bowery singer named Blind Sol. Blind Sol was glad to have Israel lead him by the arm and soon found it advisable to let the boy join him in song. The barroom music lovers must have been woefully unstrung by the old tattered troubadour and the high-voiced waif when together they ripped into *The Mansion of Aching Hearts*. Israel's share of the night's profits was often as high as fifty cents.

Now a rising wage earner, Israel rejoined his family. But he went on singing his way through waterfront, Chinatown, and Bowery saloons. His first steady job was as a singing waiter in a new Chinatown saloon known as "Nigger Mike's." This was the nickname of its swarthy Russian proprietor, who looked almost dark enough to be a Negro. Mike's colorful clientele came from the Bowery. This famous New York thoroughfare was once a throbbing center for the city's underworld. Gangsters, sailors, sports, billowy prostitutes, and uptown dudes on a slumming spree poured into its taverns, and music always poured out. Overhead ran a screeching railroad, scattering dirt and sparks on the darkened street below. Social reformers called it the tunnel to purgatory.

In this spirited setting Israel was passably content, singing popular songs and making up ribald parodies of them as he swept the sawdust floors after hours. One day consternation reigned in Mike's. In a rival saloon called Callahan's, Jerry, the waiter, and Al Piantadosi, a piano player, had written a song called *My Mariuccia Take a Steamboat*. Not only was it a smash hit with the customers, not only did it move Callahan to brag unbearably, but it was even published.

All this was galling to Mike, and something had to be done about it. Israel went right to work and wrote the words for a song which he called *Marie from Sunny Italy*. Mike's piano player, "Nick" Nicholson, picked out a tune for it, and, by good luck, the boys got it published. It was not a success. Israel's royalties were thirty-seven cents.

But *Marie* served to give the young song writer a new identity. He discarded the name Baline, because he thought it was hard to say, and on the sheet music had his name printed I. Berlin. He had privately decided that henceforth I. should stand for Irving, but feared to spell it out lest his cronies think he was putting on airs. Mike fired I. Berlin early one morning because he caught him snoozing over his broom, while the cash register had been robbed of twenty-five dollars. Years later Berlin learned that Mike had taken the money, possibly as an excuse to get rid of I. Berlin for not writing as good a song as Callahan's.

Whatever Mike thought, Berlin knew now he wanted to be a song writer. For the time being he concentrated on writing the words for songs. Finally, one of them, *Sadie Salome, Go Home*, sold 200,000

*At sixteen, the young Berlin was working as a singing waiter in a Chinatown saloon.*

*At twenty-six, Berlin was a partner in a music publishing firm.*

copies, established him so firmly as a lyricist that he was hired for twenty-five dollars a week, plus royalties on every song, by New York music publisher Ted Snyder. The year was 1909.

As the center of United States music publishing, New York with its vast mixture of foreign-born citizens had a great effect on the nation's musical diet. The city reverberated with Italian, Jewish, Irish, and German accents. Berlin wrote *Yiddisha Eyes, When You Kiss an Italian Girl,* and *Oh! How that German Could Love.* Like all song writers, he snatched titles everywhere. One of his earliest hits originated in a barbershop, when a composer friend asked him to go out on the town that night, saying, "My wife has gone to the country." Berlin shouted, "Hurrah!" The two did not go out on the town. They spent the night writing what became a tremendous American hit: *My Wife's Gone to the Country, Hurrah! Hurrah!*

The character of popular music in the early 1900s was changing rapidly from the "Tearful Nineties" when the whole singing population had a good long sozzle in glucose and gloom. Now the high spirits of an energetic nation were bubbling up. It was the heyday of vaudeville, when traveling singers and comics stopped off at the publishers' offices, begging for catchy new songs to attract their fans. After the singers had moved on, the fans rushed out to buy the sheet music, play it on their own pianos, and call in the neighbors to enjoy the whole thing over again (just as phonograph records spread the popularity of music today).

The melody factories of New York, where Berlin was writing a dozen lyrics a week, were fueled by talent from overseas. Many of the best song writers, such as Rudolf Friml, Victor Herbert, and George Gershwin, were foreign-born or first-generation Americans. They brought to United States music the grace of the Viennese operetta, the verve of the Irish jig, the emotional richness of the synagogue chant. Still another voice was joining the choir: the Negro with his "blues" and rhythm. The rhythm was called ragtime (after a Negro clog dance sometimes called "ragging"), and for years it had been shaking the wharves and bordellos of New Orleans just as it was destined to shake the nation and the world.

Berlin was captivated by the jubilant rhythm. He used it in several songs, particularly in one which he called *Alexander's Rag-time Band,* and which he first wrote without words. When he put words to it, his publishers demurred, saying that the range was too high. Berlin sang it himself at the *Friars' Frolic,* a vaudevillians' theatrical production. Still it took months for the song to gain wide popularity. But *Alexander* eventually became one of the greatest hits ever written and a landmark in American popular music.

The tune gave impetus to a dance craze that for thirty years made Americans stay up late, lose weight, and change their habits of social conduct. Preachers denounced it from the pulpit, calling it the "devil's rigadoon." It also made the composer at twenty-three very rich and internationally famous. From then on, with rare exceptions, his songs read "Words and Music by Irving Berlin."

Shortly after his triumph with *Alexander,* Berlin suffered the greatest tragedy of his life. He married the beautiful, twenty-year-old Dorothy Goetz, and they went to Cuba for their honeymoon. There she caught typhoid fever. She died in the handsome New York apartment which Berlin had provided for her to begin their married life. For months Berlin tried to overcome his grief by intense work. But the songs he wrote were spiritless and dull. Finally his wife's brother, Ray Goetz, carried Berlin away, almost bodily, to Europe in the hope that a new environment would restore his talents. Still the melody refused to flow. As a last resort, Ray offered the soundly therapeutic suggestion that Berlin try to express his sorrow deeply and openly in his music. In memory of his wife Berlin wrote *When I Lost You,* one of his loveliest ballads. Then he was able to work again.

At the time of World War I Berlin was assigned as a private to an army camp in New York. At the commanding general's request he wrote his first soldier show, *Yip, Yip, Yaphank,* which included the Berlin classic, *Oh, How I Hate To Get Up in the Morning.* This diatribe against that disturber of sweet slumber, the camp bugler, brought comfort and joy to the United States soldier whose freedom

AT LEFT: *As a World War I soldier, Berlin sang at rallies and produced a show.* BELOW: *In World War II he toured with his* This Is the Army.

to grouse has so often been his safety valve. The final lines of the chorus went:

> *Some day I'm going to murder the bugler,*
> *Some day they're going to find him dead;*
> *I'll amputate his reveille*
> *And step upon it heavily*
> *And spend the rest of my life in bed.**

One wonders what would happen to a lowly enlisted man who wrote such a song in Mr. Berlin's native Russia today.

Preening itself in postwar prosperity, America in the 1920s was in a mood to enjoy life, spend money, and loose its emotions. Scott Fitzgerald was writing *The Diamond as Big as the Ritz*. It was the era of tea dances in hotel palm gardens, and plush night clubs where the social set consorted with gangsters who were making hay out of Prohibition by making whisky out of hay.

Berlin was riding the champagne comber of success. He had written music for three editions of the famous *Ziegfeld Follies*, had started his own music publishing firm, and dreamed of having his own luxurious theater where his own musical shows could be displayed. In November 1921 the doors of the new Music Box Theatre opened, while the paint was still wet on its Georgian porticos, for the première of *Irving Berlin's Music Box Revue*. Critics were about equally impressed by the charm of the new theater—it is still one of the most inviting of New York playhouses—and the lavishness of the new review. Berlin was impressed, too, when the show grossed two million dollars. The four annual editions of the Music Box shows included fifty of Berlin's most enjoyable melodies, including *Say It With Music* and two enduring ballads, *What'll I Do* and *All Alone*.

At a dinner party in 1924 Berlin met a sparkling, self-possessed young lady named Ellin Mackay. She was an heiress to a fortune of thirty million dollars, a college girl, and a magazine writer. She and Berlin were immediately drawn to each other. After the party, he took her down to Jimmy Kelly's saloon to show her where he had

---

* © 1918 Irving Berlin.

worked as a singing waiter. For years, after the couple were married, Kelly used to boast that they had first met each other in his place. Ellin Berlin never objected to the lie. "Let Jimmy tell it," she told her husband. "He gets such fun out of it."

Ellin's tolerance was not inherited from her father. Clarence Mackay, president of the United States Postal Telegraph, was violently opposed to her marrying Berlin, both on religious and social grounds. His father, John Mackay, had come to America as a poor Scotch-Irish immigrant boy and had reaped a fabulous fortune from silver mining in Nevada. And, as often happens with Americans whose wealth has brought them high positions, the Mackays were fiercely determined that their descendants should maintain the family's newly won social eminence.

To thwart the courtship, Clarence even posted guards around his Long Island estate to keep the suitor off the premises. Ellin once confided her problems to the Prince of Wales while dancing with him at a ball given in his honor at the Mackay mansion. The prince, perhaps uniquely understanding about unconventional romances, conspired that night to hold her father in conversation while she made one of her secret phone calls to Berlin.

In an effort to make her forget Berlin, Mackay sent his daughter to Europe. But Ellin did not forget. Neither did Berlin. He wrote one of his tenderest love songs to her (*Always*) and subsequently assigned the royalties from the song to her as a gift. Even today, royalties still come in. Ellin refers to them sentimentally as "my *Always* fund."

Like the courtship, which was carried on through clandestine meetings and the help of trusted friends, the wedding was a hurried, last-minute affair. One day Berlin telephoned Ellin to meet him at New York's City Hall where he had arranged to have the ceremony performed. In the rush, Berlin forgot the two dollars to pay for the license. He borrowed it from a friend. Almost before the couple had left on their honeymoon to Europe, newspaper headlines shouted the news across the land, and two songsmiths saw fit to write an epithalamium, *When a Kid Who Came from the East Side Found a*

*Sweet Society Rose.* Mackay did not become fully reconciled to his daughter's marriage to Berlin until they presented him with a grandchild, Mary Ellin, two years later. Mackay himself later married an opera singer.

For all the differences in their background, the Berlins' marriage has turned out to be as durable as it is devoted. Mrs. Berlin says of her husband, "There is no thin ice in him. He is shy sometimes, but I have never seen him embarrassed." Having a deep, sure sense of his own identity, Berlin is not worried by social superficialities. He regarded Clarence Mackay's opposition to their marriage without rancor, diagnosing it as basically a sociological phenomenon.

Berlin is enormously proud of his wife's success as an author and eggs her on to work. In her latest book, published in 1957, *Silver Platter,* Mrs. Berlin writes of her grandmother, who married Clarence Mackay's father and reigned for a while in Paris and London as a queen of international society. This redoubtable lady, Mrs. Berlin points out, once lived on New York's lower East Side, only a few blocks from the Cherry Street home of Israel Baline.

In 1931, while America was reeling from its worst financial depression in decades, Berlin wrote a festive Broadway show, *Face the Music.* It opened in an Automat where the upper classes were spending their last pennies for coffee and pie. If the boy from Cherry Street relished the joke on his social superiors, such was the infectious nature of Berlin's humor that the joke could be relished by all. In Hollywood his successes multiplied. For a series of Fred Astaire-Ginger Rogers dancing movies (*Top Hat, Follow the Fleet*) he wrote a batch of music that brought a new note of easy charm to an industry that was puffed up with corny grandeur.

In his music Berlin for years had been giving a voice to America. But however lavishly he had bestowed his music upon his country, he felt that America had bestowed greater gifts upon him. This thought impressed him most forcibly in 1938 when he was sailing home from a trip to Europe. Hitler had just marched into Austria, Chamberlain had come home from Munich. Returning to the rela-

*Berlin received an honorary degree from Bucknell University in 1940.*

tive peace and freedom of his own country, Berlin tried to express his gratitude in a song called *Thanks, America*. But the words and music never measured up to his emotion, so he abandoned the words.

A year later he was asked to write a patriotic number for an Armistice Day broadcast by the popular songstress Kate Smith. He thought briefly of the unfinished *Thanks, America,* and then remembered another song, *God Bless America,* which he had discarded years before from *Yip, Yip, Yaphank* because it seemed to be in the wrong mood for a soldier show.

By 1939, as Europe was erupting into war, the United States mood had changed. Berlin went to work on *God Bless America,* making revisions that improved both its melody and words. Within a few weeks after its broadcast, the song had captured the country. As a simple and devout hymn of thanksgiving, it was exactly what Americans wanted to hear and sing.

Berlin was deeply moved by its success but discounted the later rumors that it might replace *The Star-Spangled Banner* as the national anthem (it did not). All profits from its sale he turned over

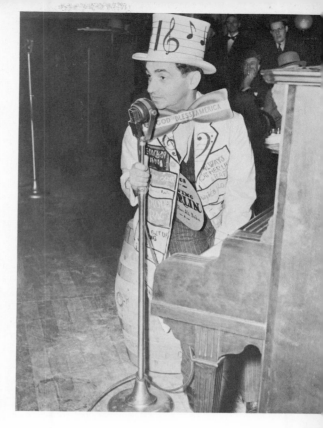

*Feted by performers' club, Berlin wore a comic costume.*

*1927 rehearsal for show produced by the late Florenz Ziegfeld (second from left) included star comedian Eddie Cantor (left), composer Berlin (at piano) and showgirls.*

*Berlin and his family are shown during 1954 ball which he attended with Mrs. Berlin (right), daughters Linda (left), and Mary Ellin.*

to the Boy Scouts and Girl Scouts of America. He appointed three old friends to administer the fund: an ex-newspaper publisher, an ex-heavyweight champion, and a United States Army general. They were, respectively, a Jew, a Catholic, and a Protestant.

When the United States entered World War II in 1941, Berlin immediately thought of writing a new soldier show. Though fifty-three, he lived the life of a soldier for two months, absorbing the mood and lingo of this new generation. After its United States and British tours, *This Is the Army* played all the theaters of war from Iran to the South Seas; and Irving Berlin went along with it, chanting his old plaint, *Oh, How I Hate To Get Up in the Morning*. In

Rome he gave one show for the benefit of an Italian charity for children. Almost nobody in the audience could speak English. But they called for his songs like *Remember* and *All Alone*. Then Berlin, to their delight, sang in Italian one of their own favorites, *Oi, Marie,* which he had learned as a youngster on the sidewalks of New York. The proceeds from *This Is the Army,* including those from the movie version, totaled ten million dollars. Berlin donated it to his country.

During the war his movie *Holiday Inn* was released, which included the song *White Christmas*. This nostalgic evocation of a snowy, old-fashioned American holiday found tremendous favor with United States soldiers overseas, and during its first weeks of publication outsold in sheet music any of Berlin's previous songs. By early 1959 it had sold 4,100,000 copies of sheet music and 25,000,000 records. Along with his *Easter Parade,* it has become a standard holiday number. It is perhaps noteworthy that these two songs, which Americans sing on the two most important Christian holidays, were written by a Jewish composer.

After his exhausting army tour, Berlin at fifty-eight bounced back to Broadway with the best score of his career for the wild West musical, *Annie Get Your Gun*. Performed from Australia to Finland, *Annie* has joined the small repertory of enduring United States musicals.

In one of *Annie's* songs, *Doin' What Comes Natur'lly,* Berlin wrote:

> *My uncle out in Texas can't even write his name,*
> *He signs his checks with X's, but they cash them*
> *just the same.**

While there is no doubt Berlin can sign checks, though he went to school only two years in his life, the fact is that he can hardly write a musical note. He sings or plays his new compositions, often over the phone, to his "musical secretary" who writes them down. He also has a habit of calling up close friends at ungodly hours of the night and trying out new tunes and lyrics. The telephone does no in-

---

* © 1946 Irving Berlin.

*Composer at work sings a new tune over the telephone to musical secretary. Piano is a special one with a keyboard that can be shifted to any desired pitch.*

justice to Berlin's voice, which always sounds as if he were singing over the phone—with a terrible connection.

Most of his life Berlin has suffered from acute nervous indigestion, worried compulsively about his work, and been a legendary insomniac. He once said after a rare good night's sleep that he was still tired because he dreamed he hadn't slept. He has tried and failed to divert his mind with hobbies. A perfectionist, he is satisfied only with professional skill. As long as he can hum, or hear melodies in his head, he cannot escape his profession.

The task of writing both words and music has been performed with distinction by remarkably few song writers: notably Berlin himself, George M. Cohan, Cole Porter, Frank Loesser, and Noel Coward. Berlin's easygoing, seemingly spontaneous marriage of words and music is achieved more often than not by painful rewriting and polishing. Once when he was on a vacation with his wife, Berlin decided to send an Easter gift to one of his three daughters, Mary Ellin, who was then ten years old. To kindle Mary Ellin's expectations, he bought a dozen postcards and mailed one to her every day, announcing in two-line verses the impending arrival of the gift. Berlin labored intensely for three days, fussing and fretting over his couplets. He had been seized by his old compulsion, and even for a little girl he found that he had to rise to the occasion and do the job well.

If Berlin had remained in Europe all his life, his career could only be a matter of conjecture. Given a musical education, he might, with his innate genius for melody, have become another Puccini. But Berlin was probably born too late to wear Puccini's mantle; the era of romantic, melodious opera was on the wane. In all probability, America was the right, the only, place for him. Through the nation's wars, depressions, boom times, dance crazes, and ragtime orgies, Berlin has written a continuous obbligato to half a century of United States history. Ever since he began to write his first songs, the immigrant from Temun has been in the throes of a musical love affair with America. It is fortunate for both the man and the nation that they met each other.

*Spyros Skouras*

*Spyros Skouras*

*I cherish my American citizenship beyond anything I possess.*

*To me this precious possession has meanings that reach across the earth and deep into the centuries.*

*The tales that reached into the hills of Greece and across the Ionian Sea, when I was a shepherd boy, made for me a dream of a golden land of opportunity beyond the seas. Now the reality excels the dream.*

*Here is a nation, rich in all the bounty and blessings of material wealth, yet abounding above all in moral and spiritual strength. Freedom is not limited; it is the freedom of the heart and the soul. This is only part of the meaning of America to me.*

*I have not only found here a truly free society, but my own career has been spent in an art and industry happily destined to be the medium of informing the world of the benefits and virtues of our way of life, without hesitating to show honestly our shortcomings.*

*I shall be eternally grateful for the good fortune that makes me an American citizen.*

*by* ROBERT COUGHLAN

# Hollywood's Extraordinary Ambassador

THERE was a time not too many years ago when Hollywood confined its film-making to sound stages located within the geographic boundaries of Beverly Hills. Behind locked studio doors, Hollywood built its own world, synthetic to be sure, but passable enough. Hollywood producers thought nothing of building a papier-mâché Eiffel Tower in a day and tearing it down a few days later in an hour to create a Malayan jungle. Today this would be unthinkable in Hollywood, which has now become the most internationally-conscious city in America.

No serious Hollywood producer today would think of filming a picture with a Parisian setting without actually going to Paris. Hollywood's camera crews are familiar sights in all corners of the world, from Rome to Nepal and from Tokyo to Monaco. At the moment fifty per cent of Hollywood's major movies are being filmed outside the United States. When Romain Gary's novel *Roots of Heaven* was made into a movie, nothing less than the wild elephant-traveled country of the French Cameroons in Africa would do for shooting the film. The Hollywood producers who once went no farther afield than Sun Valley, Idaho, to make mountain pictures today think nothing of sending stars and crews up the sides of the Alps or the Andes for a new film. So completely has the world become Hollywood's set that a United States production of the life of John Paul Jones, the great American Revolutionary naval hero, was filmed in Spain at a little village called Denia, in England at St. James's Palace and outside Parliament, in France at Versailles, and in America at Williamsburg, Philadelphia, and Annapolis. The movie was financed by a combination of United States dollars, English pounds, Italian lire, and Spanish pesetas which totaled four million dollars.

Furthermore, in the newly internationalist Hollywood, foreign actors and actresses can now become United States movie stars without setting foot in Hollywood. In the old days, it was unknown for a foreign star to enjoy top billing in an American film without first having served an apprenticeship of months, if not years, in the Hollywood studios. Not any more, at least for such foreign stars as Brigitte Bardot, Sophia Loren, Gina Lollobrigida, Maria Schell, Alec Guinness, Jack Hawkins, and Curt Jurgens, who are received in Hollywood with prestigious fanfare. The foreign stars also share equal billing with the best American actors.

But the biggest manifestation of a Hollywood gone international is what started it all in the first place: box office receipts. No Hollywood film is made today without an acute sensitivity on the part of the producer that the movie must make as much money abroad as in America (if not more) in order to show a significant profit. Indeed, of the more than two billion dollars grossed by the United States movie industry in 1958, more than half was earned in countries outside the United States where movie attendance is double that in America.

No man in Hollywood views this metamorphosis with a more benign expression than Spyros Skouras. Mr. Skouras is the president of 20th Century-Fox Film Corporation, the largest film producer in the United States. More than any other single individual, it was Skouras who led Hollywood out of its back lot isolationism into its present globe-girdling activities. Skouras was led to this decision by the crisis brought upon United States movies by television. While American movie-going was on the decline, movie-going abroad was still on the increase, and he set out to stimulate it even more.

In 1958 ten of 20th Century-Fox's twenty-five major pictures were made overseas, regardless of story locale. Twentieth Century has expanded its overseas theater holdings to Australia, Brazil, Colombia, Egypt, England, Holland, India, New Zealand, and South Africa. Typical of Skouras' productions is a 20th Century film called *The Sheriff of Fractured Jaw,* one of the most American film titles of the last ten years. The film, nevertheless, was shot in Spain and stars the distinguished English actor Kenneth More. Twentieth Century-Fox has also released a movie of a missionary in China, titled *The Inn of the Sixth Happiness.* Most of its outdoor shots were made in Wales, and the English missionary is played by Ingrid Bergman of Sweden, a particular Skouras favorite. Not only does Skouras film many of his movies outside the United States, use many foreign actors, and make most of his profits abroad, but he has even changed the movie-watching habits of the world. Most American movies today are shown on a wide screen pioneered by Skouras but invented in France. The wide-screen process, called CinemaScope, has revolutionized movie-viewing in the United States and has altered the screen of most of the 109,000 movie theaters in the rest of the world.

This wooing of the world market seems perfectly natural to Spyros Skouras, since he is an immigrant. Skouras saw America for the first time when he was seventeen years old, and his love for America and things American is second only to his love for the movies. Skouras can talk happily and at great length about the impact of his first sight of the Statue of Liberty. But for a real Skouras monologue it is only necessary to bring up some aspect, any aspect, of the movie business.

Skouras' idea of a delightful evening at home is to run off two or three feature-length films in his private projection room. He sees not only the whole output of 20th Century-Fox but that of every other major United States studio and important independent producer—a total of some three hundred features a year. Since Skouras is intensely gregarious and likes to share his pleasures, relatives and any friends within reach are dragooned for these continuous home film festivals. His daughter-in-law, hospitalized after the birth of her first child, recalls that after a while she began to feel uneasy, as if something were inexplicably but terribly wrong. She assumed that it was a form of postnatal depression until it occurred to her that something *was* wrong—she perforce had not been seeing five or six movies a week.

Skouras has the patience of a fox and the endurance of a goat when these qualities are necessary in gaining an end, but he prefers to act like a bull moose and usually does. When he charges a target, debris—and often a body or two—fills the air. Skouras means "now" when he says it, and the lapse of even a little time makes him extremely irritable. His war against time drives him to extremes that probably would kill a man with a less rugged physique. His working day ordinarily is at least twelve hours long and often as much as twenty. It begins at about 7 A.M. when, en route by car from his home in Rye, a suburb of New York City, he picks up one or more of the 20th Century-Fox executives who live in neighboring towns. He conducts business all the way to his office in the city. There he goes at once to the Turkish bath included among the comforts of his office, often trailed by an executive or two, and then to the massage table, where he begins dictating to a secretary and making telephone calls to various parts of the world. He has been known to cut the massage time in half by having two masseurs, one for each side. At the barbershop, his next stop, he continues to dictate and talk on the telephone while Ralph, the barber, beats, steams, and colognes his face. Then, nattily but conservatively dressed, he is ready for the official beginning of a supercharged day which may not end until 4 A.M.

Actually, while Skouras' nominal sleep quota is only four or five hours a night, he usually manages to accumulate another hour or so in cat naps during the day. He has an astonishing and often disconcerting ability to fall instantly and peacefully to sleep under almost any circumstance. "You've got to watch him like a hawk," one of his associates says. "You think you're having a talk with him, and all of a sudden the son of a gun's gone to sleep on you. Then he'll wake up in a minute or two feeling great and go right on." These naps are not only restorative but often protective, saving Skouras the discomfort of listening to things he would rather not hear.

Energy, driving force, shrewdness, and personal warmth would perhaps have made Skouras a success in almost any business, but what equips him particularly for show business is his colossal optimism. Misfortune merely excites him, offering as it does a fresh new challenge to meet and obstacles to be vigorously overcome. Indeed, his career from the beginning has been based on misfortune, and troubles have been spurring him on ever since.

It was bad luck in the first instance to be born (in 1893) into a family of ten children of whom half were girls, for the girls as they grew up to marriageable age needed dowries. Moreover, the Skouras farm at Skourohorion (Skourasville) was infested by "Mediterranean worm," which ruined the vineyards, and then was flooded by a burst dam, which left it covered with stones and sand. The solution was to hoard all remaining resources for the dowries and to put the four boys—one had died in infancy—to work as soon as possible. As the oldest son, Demetrios had the duty of staying on the farm to try to rehabilitate it. Charles, the next oldest, took steerage passage to America where the streets were said to be paved with gold. Spyros, next in line, was allowed to stay in a monastery school until he was thirteen and then sent off to the nearby Greek city of Patras to work as a printer's apprentice, and later as an office boy at an insurance and navigation company. He was still there when, in 1910, Charlie sent him the money for passage to the United States.

Charlie had done well in the land of opportunity. Starting as a waiter's helper at the Jefferson Hotel in St. Louis, he had risen to become a bartender and was getting about twenty-five dollars a week in tips besides his regular salary of eight dollars a week. Soon he was able to start Spyros on this same ladder with a job at the Planters Hotel. Within a year Spyros and Charlie were able to send for their youngest brother George and get him a job as well, thereby forming a team that before long developed into the greatest family act since the Medicis.

Even as a little boy in Skourohorion, Spyros had been fretted by ambition and a thirst for knowledge. St. Louis merely increased the size of his ambitions. The sixteen-hour day became a habit with him then. He arrived at the Planters at 3:45 A.M. and presented himself to Frank Balzer, the bartender. Thereupon Skouras attacked twelve big blocks of ice, pounding half into lumps for highballs and shaving the others into fine ice for cocktails. Then he swept out and prepared for the first customers at 10 A.M., after which he doubled as a waiter. Finishing at 4 P.M., he went to the Jones Commercial College where he studied accounting, commercial law, English, and shorthand. Sometimes by bedtime, he recalls, his feet were so sore that patches of skin came off with his socks. After two years at Jones he took night courses at a nearby law school, with no special desire to be a lawyer, but to equip himself as broadly as possible for a career in business.

The brothers lived frugally, walking to work from their cheap rooming house to save the five cents carfare and allowing themselves only the luxury of going to the vaudeville theaters or amusement parks on Sunday, their day off. Already they were thinking of the entertainment business as a possible target. They had a joint bank account, and by 1913 they had saved $3,500.

News of this bank roll was like catnip among the city's numerous Greek colonists and particularly interested three men who were setting up a group of coin-operated movie machines and needed extra capital to finish the project. One, a friend of Spyros', approached him with the idea that the boys should invest $3,000 for a one-fourth interest. The machines were duly set up, but before long a scale-model Peloponnesian War developed between the three Skourases and the three others, with the upshot that the former contracted to buy out the leading one of the latter, thereby giving the Skourases the controlling interest. The brothers were on their way.

Shortly they had paid this debt and saved enough besides to buy another small theater. In 1917 Spyros joined the U.S. Air Corps and was within a few months of getting his commission as a pilot when the war ended. Six months after his return the brothers signed notes to buy the West End Lyric, a first-run theater, and the Downtown Lyric and soon afterward leased six other neighborhood theaters. Everything they touched made money. By 1925 they had an interest in almost every important theater in St. Louis, as well as in most of the smaller ones, and had built the six-million-dollar,

*Spyros, Charlie and George Skouras as young men in St. Louis, 1914.*

*Skouras as an air cadet during World War I.*

seventeen-story, air-conditioned Ambassador Building housing the Ambassador Theater, a cinema palace on the grandest scale. They were famous throughout the movie industry; and Spyros was a board member and trustee of First National Pictures.

It has come about through furious application to work and what has been called their "forest instinct"—quickness to seize and press any advantage, quickness to learn from experience, an intuitive understanding of human motivation which enabled them to manipulate people—individuals, or whole audiences. From the moment a customer approached a Skouras theater he was enveloped in an atmosphere of warm solicitude. To all this the Skourases added the best entertainment they could find or invent. Their stage shows, which accompanied movies at their big houses, were the wonder of

St. Louis, and theater operators from all over the Midwest came to look at them.

Since the brothers were as intertwined as a grapevine, it was difficult to know where one began and the other left off. Nevertheless, by tacit agreement among them there was a division of functions. George, as the youngest, was a junior partner and man of all work, a role he sometimes found irksome. He was less effusive to the customers than Spyros and Charlie thought he should be, and they took him to task about it. "Listen!" he said hotly. "I will polish the brass. I will carry the film. I will sweep with the broom. But, by God, I won't smile all the time. My cheeks ache!"

Charlie, as the oldest, was the boss of the family. It was he who decided when the joint family bank account could stand the strain of new clothes and then led the expedition downtown to buy three identical blue serge suits and three identical pairs of shoes. It was he also who supervised their joint health, making sure that they ate the right foods and got plenty of rugged exercise. As soon as they could afford it and had the space they installed a wrestling mat and after hours did calisthenics and flung one another about in the Greco-Roman style. As the senior member, Charlie also had the role of cautious patriarch, checking Spyros' grandiose ambitions. Naturally this led to arguments, and since both had powerful and volatile personalities employees and bystanders were often led to expect fratricide; but it was essentially just another form of exercise for both.

Spyros' role was that of spokesman and public ambassador for the combine. As Charlie recognized, he was the most immediately likable and persuasive of them. Moreover, he had a good head for figures and had studied law, accounting, and English, all of which left Charlie in some awe of his intellect. A fact which escaped Charlie's ear (once Charlie was interrupted by the message, "Indianapolis is calling," and answered impatiently, "I got no time now to talk to no damn Greek!") was that Spyros' English was nearly incomprehensible to most people.

It has been said of Spyros in those days, "Nobody could understand him, but everybody believed him," and it was this quality, perhaps telepathically conveyed, that saved the brothers from ruin in 1923. Confronted by an effort by Paramount Pictures, then the most important producing company, to compete the Skourases out of business, Spyros enlisted the help of Sam B. Jeffries, an old customer at the Planters Hotel. Jeffries organized a group of leading citizens, financed the brothers in the purchase of a First National franchise, and helped create a situation which ultimately led to Paramount's complete capitulation. It became clear that the only way to cope with the Skourases was to merge with them. This was evident, too, to Miss Saroula Bruiglia, an American-Italian girl who had been Spyros' sweetheart since her days as a coed at Jones Commercial College. They were married to celebrate the Skouras coup.

By then the Skourases had become legendary. The key to their success in business negotiations, so it was told, was their interchangeability. A meeting with them might last all day and half the night. But after a few hours Spyros would disappear, leaving Charlie and George to carry on, and return later looking much refreshed; then Charlie would leave with the same invigorating result; then George would go. Each would have had a steam bath, a rubdown, and a nap, their opponents meantime sinking gradually into a stupor. Film salesmen approached them warily, knowing that somehow the brothers probably would maneuver them into taking less rental for their films than they asked. An associate remembers watching this happen to a man representing Harold Lloyd films, which were then selling at a very high premium. The salesman had settled on a figure with Spyros when Charlie walked in, and Spyros beamingly told him what a fine deal he had made. Charlie's face darkened and he clutched the table. "What!" he shouted. "Spyros, you are trying to bankrupt us!" It was a fine deal, Spyros insisted. An ear-shattering argument ensued. The brothers pounded the table, kicked the furniture. A chair was broken. "It was utter chaos," the friend remembers. "The Harold Lloyd guy just sat there terrified." Finally Charlie shouted, "O.K., *Mr. Skouras!* I don't call you brother any more. Go back to Greece!" charged from the office, and slammed the door. Spyros turned to the salesman and gasped, "See? I did my best." Badly

ΕΠΙ ΤΟΙΣ ΕΓΚΑΙΝΙΟΙΣ
ΤΟΥ ΠΕΡΙΛΑΜΠΡΟΥ ΝΑ-
ΟΥ ΤΗΣ ΤΟΥ ΘΕΟΥ ΑΓΙ-
ΑΣ ΣΟΦΙΑΣ ΕΝ ΛΟΣ ΑΓ-
ΓΕΛΕΣ, Η ΑΥΤΟΥ Θ. ΠΑΝΑ-
ΓΙΟΤΗΣ Ο ΟΙΚΟΥΜΕΝΙ-
ΚΟΣ ΠΑΤΡΙΑΡΧΗΣ ΑΘΗΝΑ-
ΓΟΡΑΣ Α! ΕΚΦΡΑΖΕΙ ΒΑ-
ΘΕΙΑΝ ΕΥΑΡΕΣΚΕΙΑΝ
ΤΩ, ΕΙΔΡΥΤΗ, ΑΥΤΟΥ
ΚΟΝΣΤΑΝΤΙΝΩ, Π. ΣΚΟΥΡΑ,
ΚΑΙ ΕΠΙΣΤΕΛΛΕΙ ΑΥΤΩ,
ΚΑΙ ΤΗ, ΣΥΖΗΓΩ, ΑΥΤΟΥ
ΦΛΟΡΕΝΤΙΑ,. ΤΟΙΣ ΤΕΚΝΟΙΣ
ΑΥΤΟΥ ΕΔΙΦ, ΜΑΡΓΑΡΙΤΑ,
ΚΑΙ ΚΑΡΟΛΩ,, ΤΟΙΣ
ΑΔΕΛΦΟΙΣ ΑΥΤΟΥ
ΣΠΥΡΙΔΟΝΙ Π. ΣΚΟΥΡΑ ΚΑΙ
ΓΕΟΡΓΙΩ, Π. ΣΚΟΥΡΑ, ΚΑΙ
ΠΑΣΙ ΤΟΙΣ ΣΥΝΔΡΑΜΟΥ-
ΣΙ ΦΙΛΟΙΣ ΚΑΙ ΣΥΝΕΡΓΑ-
ΤΑΙΣ ΑΥΤΟΥ ΤΑΣ ΙΕΡΑΣ
ΕΥΛΟ...

UPON THE OCCASION OF
THE DEDICATION OF THE
SAINT SOPHIA CATHED-
RAL, HIS HOLINESS THE
PATRIARCH OF CON-
STANTINOPLE ATHENA-
GORAS I, EXPRESSES
HIS DEEP GRATITUDE
TO ITS FOUNDER
CHARLES P. SKOURAS
AND SENDS HIM AND
HIS WIFE FLORENCE,
AND HIS CHILDREN
EDITH, MARGARET AND
CHARLES; HIS BROTHERS
SPYROS P. SKOURAS AND
GEORGE P. SKOURAS AND
ALL HIS ASSOCIATES, FRI...
ENDS AND CO...
THE HOLY B...
THE ORTHO...

*Cheerful givers, Spyros, Charlie and George stand before the tablet that credits them with building a Greek Orthodox Church in Los Angeles, 1952.*

*Darryl Zanuck, one-time vice-president in charge of all production for 20th Century-Fox and Mr. Skouras. Mr. Zanuck now releases his independently made films through 20th Century-Fox.*

shaken, the salesman signed with him for a much lower figure. This scene was played with variations a number of times, always with good results.

The Skourases had defeated Paramount's effort to gain captive exhibition outlets on their home grounds; now in the late '20s a similar but larger war developed, with Paramount again on the offensive. The Skourases moved into battle; a voting trust agreement with First National and its merger with the expanding Warner Brothers studios brought Spyros and George to New York City and put the brothers into nationwide operations. Then came the famous United States stock market crash of 1929. The Skourases had risen fast; they fell even faster.

Inevitably they bounced. They picked up the old Fox theater chain in New York and soon had it making money. At the request of Winthrop Aldrich of the Chase National Bank they took over Fox's bankrupt West Coast and Middle West chain. In less than three years they put it on a paying basis, and Spyros turned to the problem of the Fox studio itself, which was making poor pictures and no money. What it needed, Spyros saw, was a good executive producer —someone with originality and drive; someone like Darryl Zanuck, who had made good pictures at Warner's and now had formed 20th Century Pictures with Joseph M. Schenck. Shortly 20th Century-Fox was born, with Sidney Kent as president, Schenck as chairman of the board, and Zanuck as vice-president in charge of production. Spyros got nothing from his midwifery but the good will of those concerned, but this turned out to be important.

In 1942 Kent died, and by general acclamation Spyros was elected president of the company. At the same time Wendell Willkie became chairman of the board, the chief reason being Aldrich's belief that a big, important company such as 20th Century-Fox

*Skouras* (right), *and General James A. Van Fleet when he was Commander of the UN forces in Korea. General Van Fleet is at present a member of the Board of Directors of 20th Century-Fox.*

needed an impressive spokesman, a role in which the patrician Aldrich could not imagine Spyros. Since then, it has been observed, Spyros has made more speeches than Willkie did in the course of his whole public career, including his campaign for the presidency of the United States. Brothers Charlie and George stuck to the theater side of the business. Charlie died in 1954 at sixty-six; George is still as active as ever.

The period after his election as president of the corporation was the next great phase of Spyros' life. He became a public figure, even an international figure, not, however, because of his new position in the movies, but because for the first time he was stirred by something that seemed to him even more important than the movies. This was the plight of Greece under the Nazis and Fascists. After the Italian invasion the Greek War Relief Association, under Spyros' leadership, sent five million dollars in cash and seven million dollars in food, clothing, and medical supplies. Then the Germans attacked, Greece was completely occupied, and the Allies imposed a blockade on the country. Wide starvation resulted. Spyros—backed up by Charlie, George, and a large committee—worked indefatigably in Washington and London, and the statesmen proved no more able to withstand his tactics than had the film salesmen and competing exhibitors in St. Louis. Spyros says reminiscently, "They get exhausted, they approve it."

It is a modest summation of how Skouras wins: wearing down is only a part of the battle. Among the other factors are almost always being right and always being one of the world's truly great personal communicators.

Spyros still makes most of 20th Century's administrative decisions, but he also finds the time for his happiest role: being a symbol in the far parts of the world of the continuing vitality of the United States film industry. He is frequently overseas and often finds himself back in his native Greece. There recently a young American architect, racing through the lobby of a hotel to keep an appointment, nearly spilled the distinguished-looking Spyros on the floor. Whirling, the young American rushed back full of apologies and

*Roving ambassador for films and philanthropy, Skouras flies 150,000 miles a year. Mrs. Skouras accompanies him on long trips.*

heard in reply what is nearly a summation of the Skouras philosophy of life:

"Young man, *never* feel you have to apologize for being in a hurry!"

*Selman Waksman*

## Selman Waksman

*Selman A. Waksman's autobiography,* My Life with the Microbes, *is dedicated as follows:*

### To My Grandchildren
### Nan and Peter
#### NATIVE AMERICANS

*Your grandparents came to this country as pioneers to help build a new world. Just as earlier pioneers who came to clear the forests, cultivate the virgin land, fight the undesirable animals and transplant the desirable ones, so your grandparents came to avoid persecution, to find greater freedom, and to contribute their share in making this country a better place in which to live. They came from an old race, one that has given the world its highest code of ethics and morals; they, in turn, have tried to create more knowledge, to help alleviate human suffering, and to make the life of man a happier one. They have labored so that you will find the world perhaps somewhat freer from prejudices, freer from suffering, than they themselves have found it.*

*by* RICHARD CARTER

# *Miracle Man of the Soil*

THIS is the first age of man in which it has been possible to regard good health and long life as normal rather than accidental. Diseases that have killed countless millions of human beings are at last being controlled. All nations capable of employing modern medicine in the public behalf are achieving levels of health that would have been inconceivable before antibiotics were developed.

The turning point came during World War II, when science began to develop the antibiotics, the "wonder drugs" that actually cure bacterial disease. By poisoning hostile bacteria, either killing them outright or obstructing their malign influence on human blood and tissue, the marvelous new chemicals have become one of the most important instruments of survival in the history of mankind.

167

No man now alive has been more prominent in the discovery and improvement of the antibiotics than Selman Abraham Waksman of Rutgers University, New Brunswick, New Jersey, U.S.A., formerly Zolmin Abraham Waksman of the rural Russian Ukraine. Waksman immigrated to the United States in 1910 at the age of twenty-two and since then has become a world authority on the life processes of microbes. He is best known, of course, for the discovery of streptomycin, which is effective against the tuberculosis germ and other deadly bacteria which defy the first great antibiotic to be discovered, penicillin. In fact, streptomycin is derived from a soil-dwelling microbe that Waksman discovered in 1915 when he was still a student at Rutgers and had not yet even won United States citizenship.

The widely-used neomycin and about a dozen less celebrated antibiotics are also credited to Waksman and his collaborators in his Rutgers laboratory. One of his least-known discoveries has shown tentative promise against certain forms of cancer and is being studied with great enthusiasm by cancer investigators in Europe and America.

It is poetically appropriate that Waksman, of all people, is a dominant figure in antibiotic research. As a citizen of the United States, he personifies American concentration on the sciences of health. As an immigrant, he symbolizes the fundamentally international character of those sciences. As a specialist in both pure and applied research, Waksman has demonstrated that the differences between academic and practical science can be resolved. As an ungovernably self-reliant thinker whose work has been supported partly by government and partly by private industry, he exemplifies the dynamics of a free science in a free society.

Finally, and most appropriately in one devoted to the health of the human race, Waksman is a man of peace. With the approval of the U.S. Department of State, he has become an occasional intermediary in scientific matters between the United States and the land of his birth. He has tried to give technical help to the pharmaceutical industry of the Soviet Union, which failed at first to appreciate the importance of the antibiotics. He has arranged for the exchange of expert research personnel between the two countries. He has stressed in numerous conversations with Soviet scientific leaders the need for co-operation in matters of this sort, so that trust may become possible in other matters.

Selman Waksman was born under a thatched roof in Novaia-Priluka, a drab little trading center about two hundred miles by horse and wagon from Kiev. His mother ran an inconsequential dry-goods business. His father, the son of a coppersmith and trained as a weaver, spent most of his time studying in the sanctuary of the synagogue.

It was a life in which poverty was everywhere and the highest realizable aspirations were those of the spirit. The Bible and Talmud were the bases of all significant knowledge, all culture. There were no free schools open to the whole population. For a Jew, secular education usually consisted of learning the family trade and learning how to defend oneself in case of a pogrom. Relations with the peasants were limited to commerce and, for the boy, to street fights.

Human stamina and love of home and family being what they are, Waksman remembers his drab childhood as a time of great love and unselfishness. His mother made extraordinary sacrifices to provide him with an education, not because she hoped that he would become rich and famous but because she prayed that he would become a man of wisdom. By the age of five he was in a *heder,* or private religious school, learning to read the Bible and memorizing the daily prayers. At seven he was working his way through the intricacies of the Talmud, developing the capacity for intense concentration on detail that later was to serve him—and much of mankind—so well. At nine he was entrusted to tutors, Jews who had managed to get a general education for themselves. With their help he began to learn Russian literature, history, arithmetic, and geography.

The sense of group responsibility so often found among the oppressed was highly developed in young Waksman. What he learned from his threadbare teachers he passed on to others, as an unpaid tutor in an unlicensed school that was raided at regular intervals by

*Young Waksman on the eve of his departure for the United States, 1909.*

the police. The main interest of the police was bribes, rather than the enforcement of the Czar's anti-Semitic laws. The teen-age boy and his fellow conspirators in grammar and history paid the bribes and continued their studies.

Waksman never attended secondary school. A rigid system of religious quotas barred most Jews from the gymnasiums which were virtually the only institutions in which an adequate secondary education could be obtained. However, anyone who could learn enough to pass month-long competitive examinations could win a document certifying that his knowledge was equivalent to that acquired in a gymnasium.

In 1907, prepared as well as possible by inexpert private instruction and voracious study, the nineteen-year-old Waksman went to Zhitomir for an examination covering the first five years of the eight-year curriculum. He passed with high marks in literature and languages but failed his favorite subject, geography. He failed, much to the delight of the popinjay who examined him, because he did not know the name of the river that flows through Berlin (the Spree). He was summarily flunked.

Waksman refused to abandon his program. To him, knowledge was an end in itself and examinations were of no consequence. But to enter a university and get all the additional knowledge that he craved, he needed gymnasium accreditation. Accordingly, he returned home, replenished his funds, and studied as if his life depended on the outcome. In 1909 he took the seventh-year examination at Odessa, to avoid his tormentor of the previous tests. He passed. Within a year he was ready for the eighth-year examinations; but now he was turned away because of a new decree admitting only those who had been born in Odessa or had lived there twenty years. Waksman was more than ever determined not to be stopped. He convinced an "unscrupulous" minor government official to issue him a certificate of residence. He then passed the examinations and was given his credentials.

But now, his battle won, Waksman decided to leave Russia anyway. His mother had died shortly before he had taken his final examination. Young Waksman's ties to the town of Priluka had died with her. He could now go as far afield as his limited funds could take him. And he felt that the farther afield he could get, the better.

Some of his cousins had immigrated to the United States, and they had written glowingly of the opportunities there. One was a farmer near Metuchen, New Jersey, and offered to put Waksman up if he would come. The young man had no particular interest in farming, but he was anxious to study science. He had never been in a scientific laboratory in his life, but he now decided that he would go to the United States and study biology or medicine.

In October 1910, with four other emigrants, Waksman left Priluka by train for the German border. "We have shaken the shackles off our feet," they shouted with revolutionary fervor. "We are entering upon a new world, a free world, where man is free."

Waksman traveled in the steerage of an ocean liner from Bremen and was put ashore at Philadelphia on November 2, 1910. He remembers riding goggle-eyed atop his baggage in a horse-drawn carriage. He remembers the jokes that his cousins made about him—the new arrival, the greenhorn. He remembers being gorged on good food and being filled with a sense of adventure and being troubled that he knew no English. He developed a working grasp of the language in months, but even today he still speaks with a faint Russian accent.

He lost no time in applying for enrollment in one of America's great medical schools, the College of Physicians and Surgeons at Columbia University in New York City. On the basis of his hard-won gymnasium certificate, the medical school accepted him. But he could not get scholarship aid and he had no money. Relatives offered to assist with his tuition and living expenses, but he refused. "Already I was becoming saturated with the spirit of the New World," he says. "I had a deep desire to depend on myself."

He had met Dr. Jacob G. Lipman, head of the Bacteriology Department at the College of Agriculture at Rutgers. Lipman was also a Russian immigrant and understood the young man's ambitions. He told Waksman that an agricultural curriculum would lay a good foundation. So Waksman applied for a scholarship at nearby Rutgers and won it in a state-wide competitive examination. He had been in the United States only about six months.

In 1911 Waksman entered the college and for the first time in his life sat down as a full-fledged student in a duly authorized secular classroom. He was ill at ease in the new environment, but he was accustomed to unease. At first he was a campus joke—a small, solemn man among rawboned American adolescents, a Talmudic intellectual among devotees of the football bleachers.

"They used to laugh at my accent," he says. "Once I had to pronounce a mathematical formula that contained the letters 'OL.' I pronounced them 'Oh Hell' and brought down the house. But there was no malice in the laughter. They were just boys, and even though I thought they were lamentably frivolous I soon realized that I had a good deal to learn from them. All my learning was book learning, but they had been living full lives and had far more practical knowledge than I had."

He soon won the respect of his classmates by his solemn devotion to study, his patient good humor and, not least, his discourses in the literature classes on such subjects as "The Insulted and Repressed Types in Russian Literature," novel and impressive concepts for an American agricultural college. In his third year he augmented his scholarship aid with a job, which paid twenty cents an hour. It consisted of assisting in experiments at the college farm. He no longer needed to live on his cousin's farm. Now he was fully independent, in a $3-a-month room, eating cracked eggs that he bought for eleven cents a dozen.

Besides income, his new job gave him opportunities to study the fundamental laws of genetics and plant nutrition, a great addition to his growing knowledge of soil chemistry. It was during this period that he was learning to mistrust some of the conventional teachings about the nature of soil. According to accepted doctrine, the only microbes of any significance in the soil were the bacteria and fungi. But Waksman kept encountering other organisms that belonged to neither group.

"They are a kind of bacteria," said a professor.

"They are nothing of the kind," thought Waksman.

They were strangely beautiful creatures, with long tendrils and many colors. He found that others before him had noticed them and had even given them a class name: *actinomyces*. Little was known of their chemistry or of the role they played in the silent, microscopic world of the soil. Waksman evidently did not have to learn a great deal about them to know more than any other human being. He set out to become an expert, little dreaming that various types of actinomycetes would some day become the sources of virtually every major antibiotic in the world.

Many of Waksman's professors could not keep up with him and did not even try. He was, after all, an undergraduate in an agricultural college and was showing little interest in animal husbandry or other bucolic pursuits. His insistence on prowling in the loneliness of the unknown hardly could have ingratiated him to men whose main interest was the practical application of existing knowledge.

Some professors were, of course, far more understanding. Throughout his college career Waksman enjoyed the warm support and patient guidance of men who shared his unconventional but thoroughly scientific conviction that knowledge need not have immediate practical value to be of significance. These men encouraged the intense young Russian's feeling that science could ill afford to remain ignorant of the biology and chemistry of the very earth on which man walks and from which he draws sustenance. If the friendly professors feared occasionally that Waksman was headed up blind alleys, they withheld criticism. They felt, as he felt, that his dedication to learning needed to be cherished and cultivated.

For that era, Waksman's views were indeed weird. He saw a spoonful of earth not as a glob of dirt but as a miniature world with a population of hundreds of millions of living organisms. Under his microscope the dirt burst into life as rich and colorful and violent as any jungle. Before his eyes infinitesimal creatures, vividly beautiful, contended with each other for survival in a mindless chemical warfare that had been going on since the moment of creation and would never end. His task was to learn the secrets of the combatants. But first he had to learn what the combatants were. He spent every spare minute isolating and cataloguing new groups of microbes and telling himself that humanity would profit from all this some day, in some way.

Although he concentrated on his private research he did well enough in his other studies to become a member of Phi Beta Kappa, the American academic honor fraternity. After graduation, he remained on the Rutgers campus for an additional year, continuing to study his actinomycetes, working as an assistant in the New Jersey Agricultural Experiment Station (a state-subsidized research center), and accumulating credits for a Master of Science degree. In 1916, by which time he had already published his first learned paper on the fungi and actinomycetes of the soil, he was awarded the degree. He also was granted United States citizenship. And he married a girl from Priluka. Her name was Deborah Mitnik, but he called her by the endearing nickname "Bobili," and still does.

The University of California had offered him a fellowship, which meant that he could obtain more training in chemistry, especially biochemistry, essential to his pursuit of microbiology. Accordingly, with all their possessions in two suitcases, the Waksmans entrained for Berkeley, California, the day after their wedding. Bobili is a vivacious person whose love for her now-famous husband is still uncontaminated by awe. "I had a new hat," she recalls, "an absolute dream, blue velvet with a tiny yellow veil. When we got on the train I put the hat ever so tenderly on the seat beside me. Selman came in and sat down on it."

There were some fifty other Russian emigrants at Berkeley,

*Waksman and his fiancée, Bobili, just before their marriage in 1916.*

including Bobili's brother, Peisi, who was Waksman's dearest friend. When the czarist government fell in 1917 and it seemed that democracy would be established under Alexander Kerensky, all the campus Russians except the Waksmans left for home.

"I had two reasons for remaining in the United States," says Waksman. "The first was that I liked it here. The other was that I was going to get my Doctor of Philosophy degree in another six months. It would have been foolish to discontinue my scientific training at such a point."

Bobili observes, "The ones who went back had stronger ties to Russia. Selman is not sentimental."

Waksman replies, "Not sentimental? I am so. When it is necessary, I am sentimental."

In July 1918 the young couple returned to New Brunswick. The new Doctor of Philosophy in biochemistry took up a double position as lecturer in soil microbiology at the college and microbiologist of the New Jersey State Agricultural Experiment Station. Gross income: $1,500 a year.

Designation as a microbiologist was a triumph for Waksman. The conventional title was "bacteriologist," because only bacteria were conceded any importance. The actinomycetes, fungi, and other micro-organisms were regarded as much less significant. In helping to change this erroneous conception, Waksman had to be more than a scientific investigator; he had to be a missionary. Also, to avoid offense to his scientific elders and betters, he had to be a diplomat.

He was both. Stubbornly but politely, he continued to press his arguments at scientific meetings and in scientific journals. Little by little, recognition came to him. His authoritative monographs on the biochemistry of humus, composts, and peat were widely published. His huge textbook, *Principles of Soil Microbiology,* became a classic study in the field. By the late thirties, Waksman was Professor Waksman, a figure of eminence in the scientific world.

Students came from all over the world to attend his lectures and assist in his investigations. He glowed in their adulation and felt that they were as important to his education as he was to theirs.

In one sense it was like the old days in Priluka when he learned what he could and passed on the knowledge to others. But far greater triumphs for Professor Waksman were on the horizon.

In describing what his generations of students have meant to him he loves to say: "I owe a lot to my teachers. They taught me well. . . . I owe more to my friends, because they encouraged me to continue my search for knowledge. . . . Most of all, however, I owe to my students; they continuously questioned me; they made me re-examine and re-evaluate my ideas . . . it is they who will continue the search for knowledge after I have passed away."

Of all his students, the one who made the deepest impression on Waksman and the world was René J. Dubos, a Frenchman who came to Rutgers in 1924 and spent most of his three years there working with Waksman on a study of the decomposition of cellulose by soil bacteria. After Dubos won his Ph.D., Waksman recommended him to the Rockefeller Institute, whose directors wanted a bright young investigator to look for a microbe that might be antagonistic to the pneumonia germ. In 1932, Dubos accomplished the then-unbelievable feat of isolating a soil bacterium that produced an enzyme that digested the pneumonia organisms. The possibilities for human medicine were immense.

Waksman recognized these possibilities. He saw that the time was fast approaching when science could marshal germ against germ in behalf of man's health. In 1932, at the request of the National Research Council and the Tuberculosis Association, he had undertaken a study of the fate of tuberculosis germs in the soil. In his lectures at Rutgers and elsewhere he was now making references to the strange ability of some microbes to overwhelm others by excreting chemicals. He prophesied to his audiences that their health would benefit from the phenomenon some day.

Actually, Waksman was echoing some of the predictions of Louis Pasteur, who had demonstrated the germ theory of disease during the latter half of the nineteenth century, had observed the death of pathogenic bacteria in the soil, and had said, "These facts justify the highest hopes for therapeutics." In 1901 Rudolf Em-

merich and Oscar Low of the University of Munich had extracted
pyocyanase, a potent antibacterial medicine, from a certain microbe
and had even treated patients with the stuff. But pyocyanase had
been ahead of its time. It was too unreliable for general use; biochemistry, 1901 vintage, had no means of producing it in adequate
quantity or consistent quality.

Since then, aside from Dubos' discovery of a bacterium that
could victimize the pneumonia germ, nothing much besides pyocyanase had happened to verify Pasteur's prediction. In 1928, to be
sure, Alexander Fleming of London had noted that an air-borne
mold could inhibit the growth of the germ that causes boils. Out of
curiosity, Fleming had identified the chemical with which the mold
performed the chore. He called the chemical penicillin and went
on to other work.

The big break-through in what Waksman himself was later
to call "antibiotics" (substances antagonistic to the life processes of
disease germs) came in 1938 when Dubos found in specially enriched
soil a bacterium active against several disease germs. He isolated
the organism's two pertinent chemicals and combined them in a
drug which he called tyrothricin.

Tyrothricin was the first significant antibiotic since pyocyanase.
It was dangerous for internal consumption but was effective on open
wounds and, most important of all, it showed the scientific world
that no further time should be lost in seeking medicines of microbial
origin. The sulfa drugs were already in use but had fallen short of
the ideal. They cured some diseases, but not enough. Also, they
were sometimes poisonous to the patient.

Among the scientists encouraged by Dubos' discovery were
Howard W. Florey and Ernst B. Chain of Oxford. They resurrected
Fleming's penicillin, tried it in human illnesses during 1941, and
found it incredibly effective. The great difficulty was production
during wartime. The chemical was impossibly expensive to produce
by traditional methods and also was discouragingly unstable. In
hopes that the problem could be solved soon enough to save lives
during World War II, Florey came to the United States.

Scientists and technologists of the U.S. Department of Agriculture and the American pharmaceutical industry were interested in penicillin and its implications. Florey got prompt co-operation. Within months the Americans had found a new strain of *penicillium* mold that yielded quantities of penicillin two hundred times more profuse and far more potent and stable than the original chemical. Industrial experts in biochemical engineering learned how to mass produce it. By D-Day in World War II medical corpsmen carried penicillin ashore. By the end of the war, American pharmaceutical laboratories were turning out enough vials of the drug to treat seven million patients a year and were expanding their facilities at a rate which now makes penicillin available to the sick and injured of all nations.

Selman Waksman was one of the most interested observers of this development. But he did not directly participate in the penicillin experiments, preferring to follow his own paths of discovery. In 1939, partly on the insistence of René Dubos and mainly because he considered the young Frenchman's success as proof that the time was ripe, he had set forth to find antibiotics of his own. He was immersed in the work long before Florey and Chain demonstrated the effectiveness of penicillin. Subsidized mainly by the New Jersey Agricultural Experiment Station and the pharmaceutical manufacturing firm, Merck & Co., he had turned to his old friends, the actinomycetes. From decades of observation he felt positive that these organisms would be the richest source of antibiotics.

He was right. To prove himself right he exercised the same unyielding self-discipline and implacable stubbornness that had earned him a gymnasium certificate and had made him a microbiologist instead of an orthodox bacteriologist. He collected hundreds of soil samples from which he and his students isolated thousands of microbial cultures. Each culture was subjected to systematic tests in which its ability to overcome disease bacteria was closely observed. Cultures that showed promise were purified and retested and, if they continued to show antibacterial activity, their chemistry was explored.

By 1940 the first Waksman antibiotic was at hand. It was actinomycin, produced by an organism which he dubbed *Actinomyces antibioticus*. "The drug had a remarkable ability to destroy microbes," he says, "but it was almost as good at destroying the animals we tried it on. Merck must have sacrificed ten thousand mice before we concluded that actinomycin was simply too toxic for medical use. It has since been modified, however, and has caused some excitement when tried in certain kinds of cancer. I'm working on it again."

Soon after actinomycin came clavacin and fumigacin, both of which were impressive on first acquaintance but failed to survive rigorous testing. Then, in 1942, the Rutgers workers found streptothricin, which seemed useful beyond all imagination. It had a murderous effect not only on the same disease germs that were sensitive to penicillin in the laboratory tests and clinical trials of that period but also on germs that were resistant to penicillin. When given to experimental animals it made them well and seemed to have no serious side effects.

For a short while Waksman allowed himself to think that he had made a historic discovery. And then the bad news arrived: streptothricin was deadly. Something in its chemistry undermined the chemistry of the animal patients, killing them by delayed action after it had apparently cured their bacterial diseases.

Waksman went right back on the search. He was positive that the next day or the next month or the next year would bring him the pinch of soil in which would be found the drug he had been seeking. He and his students continued to screen microbial cultures.

The big day finally did come in August 1943. From two strains of *Streptomyces griseus,* which had been one of Waksman's earliest actinomycete discoveries in 1915, the scientific team extracted a chemical as potent as streptothricin and far less toxic. Waksman gave the new chemical a name that has since become world-renowned: streptomycin.

This is all told so easily and the results of the discovery are so easily taken for granted that one might tend to underestimate what

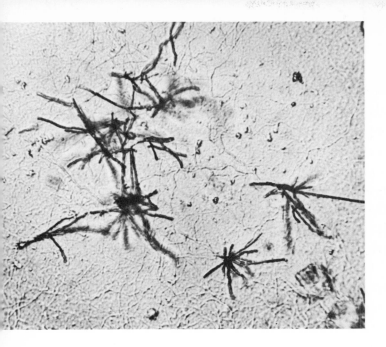

Streptomyces griseus, *the organism which produces streptomycin. A copy of this photograph hangs on the wall opposite Dr. Waksman's desk at the Institute of Microbiology.*

*Dr. Waksman* (left) *inspecting construction of the Merck streptomycin plant, Elkton, Virginia, 1946.*

Waksman and his students had accomplished. In four years they had found five antibiotics, of which one was clearly an epochal contribution to medicine. The feat was comparable to finding five needles, including one of pure gold, while picking through an infinite number of haystacks. The mathematical odds against achieving anything of this sort by random methods of investigation would have been impossibly high. Waksman's results depended almost entirely on his encyclopedic knowledge of the actinomycetes and his ability to tell when the laboratory performance of a new strain was interesting enough to warrant closer observation. This knowledge shortened to years a search that probably would have taken decades.

The most exciting characteristic of streptomycin was its potency against tuberculosis germs. No other drug had ever shown such activity. Moreover, streptomycin was able to control other pencillin-resistant bacteria such as those of whooping cough, dysentery, typhoid, plague, cholera, undulant fever, and certain varieties of pneumonia.

Merck & Co. immediately undertook a crash program of experimentation to establish the potency and safety of the drug, refine its chemistry to the maximum, and learn how to manufacture it at the most economical cost in the largest possible quantities. Less than a year after the drug was isolated in Waksman's laboratory, it was being used to arrest experimental tuberculosis at the famous Mayo Clinic. Before the end of 1944, it was being given to a few human patients. By 1946 it was in international use and had been the subject of thousands of professional articles in the learned publications. The fame of Selman Waksman was no longer confined to scientific circles. He was now a public figure.

He was showered with honors and his gratification mounted with each new acknowledgment of his importance. He also was showered with riches, but found the money an intolerable embarrassment. Under the contract between Rutgers and Merck in 1938-39, the drug company was sole proprietor of streptomycin and any other patentable discovery made in Waksman's laboratory. In return, the university was collecting 2½ per cent of the company's proceeds from sales of the drug (these sales eventually reached $50,000,000 a year). The university was giving one-fifth of its share to Waksman.

He was becoming a rich man, practically overnight, but the process was repugnant to him. He felt that he had sullied his scientific principles by permitting a single firm to control the production and marketing of a drug so important to the health of the world.

*Sir Alexander Fleming* (right), *discoverer of penicillin, was Dr. Waksman's guest at Rutgers University in 1949. Together they examined the cultures which led to the discovery of streptomycin.*

The university was also being placed in an unfavorable light. So Waksman asked Merck to relinquish its exclusive rights to the drug and permit the university to license any qualified pharmaceutical manufacturer to produce it. Merck agreed, thereby giving up millions of dollars in profits.

The situation became complicated again in 1950 when a former student who had worked on the development of streptomycin sued for recognition as its co-discoverer and asked to be awarded a share of the financial benefits. Waksman was deeply offended at the implication that he was not entitled to full credit for what he regarded as his life's work. His immediate reaction was for the university to fight the case. Then he found that, until the litigation was concluded, the university would be unable to proceed with plans for using royalty money in construction of an Institute of Microbiology which he hoped would become his monument. He saw himself spending his declining years in courts of law instead of in his Institute. He feared that his accomplishments would be dirtied and his reputation lost. He urged the university to settle the case as best it could and get on with construction of the Institute.

The former student, Dr. Albert Schatz, was given a share of the royalties, plus the title "co-discoverer." Waksman insisted on rewards for everyone else who had been working in his laboratory on the development of the antibiotics program which led to streptomycin. Thus fourteen persons involved in this work are now paid royalties. Twelve others, including the widow of the laboratory dishwasher, were given cash bonuses.

Waksman is no longer embarrassed by wealth, chiefly because he has given most of it away. Nearly eighty-five per cent of the royalties go to the Rutgers Research and Educational Foundation for the support of the Institute of Microbiology. Of his own small share, half goes to the support of a Foundation for Microbiology, which promotes his favorite science by means of research grants and scholarships. He also has established a fund which enables immigrants or the sons or daughters of immigrants to study agriculture at Rutgers. His wife has endowed Douglass College in New Brunswick (formerly the New Jersey College for Women) with a fund that provides two $500 annual scholarships to promising music students. Half of all the streptomycin royalties due Waksman from Japanese manufacturers go to a Japanese Waksman Foundation that supports microbiological research in that country. "In 1945," Waksman says, "there were not a dozen laboratories in the world with any interest in the actinomycetes. Now there are thousands."

He is a proud and happy man. If his scientific reputation was briefly shadowed by the 1950 lawsuit, the shadow was dispelled in 1952 when he was awarded the Nobel Prize for Physiology and Medicine. The pomp and ceremony thrilled him, and the warmth with which he was congratulated by his scientific peers moved him deeply. Yet he says with unmistakable conviction that the most moving and, to him, the most significant event of his triumphal trip to Sweden was the visit to his hotel of a little girl, Eva Hallstrom, who had been saved from tubercular meningitis by streptomycin.

"Before streptomycin," he says, "children never recovered from tubercular meningitis, and now they live. In Madrid, in Moscow, in Tokyo, in Paris, I have seen healthy children who would have been dead if there had been no streptomycin. I have been embraced by them and by their mothers and even by their physicians. Could there be any greater reward for me?"

Waksman is a rumpled, suitably professorial type in whom the ceremonial modesty of the scientist defers to an exuberant sense of self-satisfaction. He enjoys every aspect of his life and fame. He beams about his Nobel Prize, his fifteen honorary degrees from important universities throughout the world, his numerous acts of charity, his handsome wife, his son on the faculty of Harvard Medical School, the prominence of dozens of his former students, and, above all, the knowledge that when he pronounces judgment on a microbe or an antibiotic, the scientific world keeps quiet and listens.

He lives in hyperactive retirement near Rutgers, the scene of his growth and triumph, and does whatever he pleases. What pleases him most is to keep working. At about 7:45 A.M., five days a week,

*Dr. Waksman receiving the Nobel Prize for Physiology and Medicine from King Gustav VI of Sweden in 1952.*

he puts on a gray felt ruin of a hat, emerges from his house, climbs into a new Buick and drives, sometimes on the proper side of the road and sometimes not, to his sanctum in the $3,500,000 Institute of Microbiology that was built with antibiotic royalties. The huge building is in all respects a monument to his work, just as he hoped it would be, and he could not be more candid than he is in his pride in it.

In his comfortable offices and laboratories he attends to his cancer investigations, dictates a sequel to his already published autobiography, writes articles (some of them testy) for learned journals, and picks and chooses among the hundred prayerful invitations sent every year by institutions all over the world, asking to honor him and hear his words.

That he no longer is in active command of the Institute does not trouble him at all. Unlike the stereotyped old academician who embarrasses all hands by resisting retirement from routine administrative and teaching duties, Waksman revels in his freedom and says with conviction, "I've earned it."

Although nobody can deny that he has indeed earned his freedom and his fame, Waksman has his detractors. Some of his associates, past and present, feel that he overdoes his performance as grand old man, is too brusque in his capacity as supreme authority and too concerned with his place in scientific history. Not everyone who knows him feels that way, however, and nobody suggests that his place in scientific history is not assured. The criticisms are entirely personal.

Since he enjoys being liked and is quick to sense rebuff, he cannot forget that the only big country from which he received no congratulations after the announcement of his Nobel Prize was Russia. In 1946 he had been lionized in Moscow, where the government health officials were using every grain of streptomycin they could lay hands on. Since then Waksman's relations with the Russian government and its scientists have varied according to the ebb and flow of the cold war.

"In 1946, some important Soviet ministers got me into a room and asked me why they had failed to make penicillin," he recalls. "It was an easy question to answer but I dared not answer it. They could have had penicillin for the asking during the war and had disdained it. They could have manufactured it themselves but were handicapped partly by their emphasis on other forms of technology and mainly by party-line politics. How could I tell them that science and technology have to be left alone and can't always conform to the needs of a political party? I could not even describe to them the elementary defects of their technology. If I had told the truth the guilty politicians would have made scapegoats of some of my scientific friends."

He had been back to Russia a few times since then and, after several attempts, managed to extract an invitation to establish an exchange program under which one of his top assistants spent six months in Russia and a Russian researcher spent six months at Rutgers. Waksman believes that Russian pharmacy and medicine will probably improve to the degree that the government continues to sanction such scientific interchange.

"If something new isn't Russian they don't trust it," he says. "When I wrote that the so-called new Russian antibiotic albomycin was really grisein, one of our discoveries at Rutgers, I hurt their feelings terribly. Why should feelings of that kind have any place in science? There is no such thing as Russian science and no such thing as American science. Science is science and is international. No nation can wall off its science without hurting itself and the rest of the world."

This spirit governs his Institute of Microbiology. When the Institute was dedicated in 1954, he expressed the feeling in language which has been inscribed on a bronze plaque in the building lobby. Waksman makes sure that all his visitors read the plaque, which is pictured below. It reads:

"The Institute will devote its efforts to the study of the smallest forms of life, the microbes, wherever they are found and no matter what their activities may be. Let this Institute serve as a center where scientists from all parts of the world may gather to work, to learn, and to teach. The halls of this Institute are dedicated to the free pursuit of scientific knowledge for the benefit of all mankind.

Selman A. Waksman"

# Photograph Credits

**IGOR SIKORSKY**
*To the New World for New Wings*

14, Alfred Eisenstaedt for LIFE International; 18, 21, 22, 27, 31, Courtesy Igor Sikorsky.

**FELIX FRANKFURTER**
*A Tireless Quest for Justice*

34, Arnold Newman; 39, 40, Courtesy Felix Frankfurter; 45, Hans Knopf and Kurt Severin; 50, Acme Newspictures Inc.; 51, 53, Associated Press.

**HELENA RUBINSTEIN**
*High Priestess of American Beauty*

56, Alfred Eisenstaedt for LIFE International; 63, Peter A. Juley & Son; 66, Courtesy Helena Rubinstein; 69, Leonard McCombe.

**DALIP SAUND**
*From Chhajalwadi to the United States Congress*

74, Edward Clark for LIFE International; 81, Painting by Emile

Kosa, Jr.; 85, T. S. Satyan; 86, (top) United States Information Service, (bottom) Noel Clark from Black Star; 89, J. R. Eyerman.

### GIAN CARLO MENOTTI
*Renaissance Man of American Music*

90, Alfred Eisenstaedt for LIFE International; 95, 96, 98, Courtesy Gian Carlo Menotti; 105, 107, David Lees for LIFE International.

### DAVID DUBINSKY
*Pacemaker for Labor*

108, Alfred Eisenstaedt for LIFE International; 114, 117, 120, Courtesy ILGWU; 123, New York Daily News.

### IRVING BERLIN
*Mr. "Words and Music"*

126, Alfred Eisenstaedt for LIFE International; 133, (top) no credit, (bottom) Brown Brothers; 136, (top) European, (bottom) David E. Scherman; 140, 141 (top), Acme Newspictures; 141 (bottom), © Price Picture News; 142, New York Journal-American Photo from United Press International; 144, Cornell Capa from Magnum.

### SPYROS SKOURAS
*Hollywood's Extraordinary Ambassador*

146, Alfred Eisenstaedt for LIFE International; 155, 156, 161, Courtesy Spyros Skouras; 159, George Silk; 160, Allan Grant from "Exhibitor"; 163, Géo-Grono, Paris.

### SELMAN WAKSMAN
*Miracle Man of the Soil*

164, Alfred Eisenstaedt for LIFE International; 170, Courtesy Selman Waksman; 175, Knickerbocker Photo Studio; 181, (top) F. J. Higgins, (bottom) Merck & Co., Inc.; 183, Associated Press; 186, United Press International.